THE
TEACHING
OF
ETHNIC DANCE

This is a volume in the Books for Libraries collection

DANCE

See last pages of this volume for a complete list of titles.

THE
TEACHING
OF
ETHNIC DANCE

ANATOL M. JOUKOWSKY

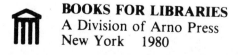
BOOKS FOR LIBRARIES
A Division of Arno Press
New York   1980

Editorial Supervision: Janet Byrne

———

Reprint Edition 1980 by Books for Libraries, A Division of Arno Press Inc.

Copyright © 1965 by J. Lowell Pratt & Company, Inc.

Reprinted by permission of Charles E. Merrill Publishing Company

Reprinted from a copy in the Charles Holbrook Library at the Pacific School of Religion

DANCE
ISBN for complete set: 0-8369-9275-X
See last pages of this volume for titles.

Manufactured in the United States of America

———

Library of Congress Cataloging in Publication Data

Joukowsky, Anatol M
    The teaching of ethnic dance.

    (Dance)
    Reprint of the ed. published by J. L. Pratt, New York, which was issued in series: New designs in physical education.
    1. Folk dancing--Study and teaching. I. Title. II. Series.
[GV1743.J65 1980]   793.3'1'07   79-7768
ISBN 0-8369-9296-2

THE
TEACHING
OF
ETHNIC DANCE

THE

TEACHING

OF

ETHNIC DANCE

MACEDONIA	BULGARIA	POLAND
GREECE	RUMANIA	RUSSIA
SERBIA	CZECHOSLOVAKIA	UKRAINE
	FRANCE	

by

ANATOL M. JOUKOWSKY

ASSOCIATE PROFESSOR OF PHYSICAL EDUCATION

SAN FRANCISCO STATE COLLEGE

Illustrated by SERGE SMIRNOFF

J. Lowell Pratt and Company

PUBLISHERS   NEW YORK

JACKET DESIGNED BY JULIO GRANDA

FOREWORD

For those of us in the field of physical education who have grown to love dance, this is a long-awaited collection. Anatol Joukowsky is established as a world renowned expert in ethnic dance. The people who have attended his workshops, particularly on the West Coast, know of his high standards, his personal and professional integrity, his ability to analyze, his first-hand knowledge of the countries and the native dances, his ability to touch each whom he teaches with a bit of his own humor, his own joie de vivre.

As Eleanor Wakefield[1] suggests, in an article in *Impulse,* 1956, Anatol Joukowsky and his talented wife, the great Yugoslavian ballerina Yania Wassilieva, emigrated to the United States in 1951. They arrived in New York direct from France after having had fascinating lives centered not only in artistic circles but political ones as well.

Professor Joukowsky was born in the Ukraine. His father was a colonel in the cavalry of Emperor Nicholas II. After World War I his family settled in Salonika, Greece. His parents wanted him to have a Slavic education so he attended school in Yugoslavia. It was in Belgrade that the ballet master of the state theatre suggested that Anatol should have dance lessons. At the age of 14 he began a two year term of ballet study. His interest grew and when Pavlova visited a school performance she singled him out for special commendation. This aided materially in his decision to make dance a career. Subsequently, however, he studied engineering at the University of Belgrade, but never

---

[1]Eleanor E. Wakefield, "Anatol Joukowsky — Teacher and Dancer," *Impulse,* 1956, p. 17.

v

gave up studying ballet. Concurrently he attended the Yugo-slavian State Theatre Ballet School and graduated in 1926. In 1935 Professor Joukowsky was named choreographer and director of the ballet for the State Theatre of Belgrade.

During 1936 Professor Joukowsky organized a small professional group to specialize in ethnic dance. This group performed at a Sokol festival in Prague in 1938. His performers won the first prize in the competition. He was not only permitted but encouraged by the director of the State Theatre to repeat the performance under its auspices. In March 1941 his first exhibition of ethnic dances at the State Theatre of Belgrade was presented. It was entitled *The Book of Yugoslavia* and provided the entreact for two ballets choreographed by Joukowsky. Mr. Joukowsky's works were enormously well received in Belgrade.

During this period Yania Wassilieva, whom Anatol Joukowsky had married in 1932, was an active participant in many of the performances, and in the scientific hunts which took them into the native hills and country-sides to find authentic dances, notating music and photographing the natives in costume. During the interim between the two world wars Professor Joukowsky was the only professional choreographer who was doing this research, and this was the last era when these dances could be found alive in these particular countries. At the end of World War II Yania performed with him in programs staged by the Special Services Division of the French Army to which Anatol Joukowsky was attached. Later, they both joined de Basil's Ballet Russe Company and toured with them for two years. Anatol Joukowsky was dancer and choreographer.

Those who have felt the impact of this remarkable man's personality and ability welcome this unusual collection of dances which Professor Joukowsky makes available for the first time under one cover. These dances come directly from the countries involved. They have been brought to the United States of America by Mr. Joukowsky. They represent authentic versions of these dances.

Mr. Joukowsky has danced in every country in Europe and

the Middle East. In addition to his many accomplishments he has been awarded the Cavalier Cross of Bulgaria from King Boris III, in 1938; the Order of St. Vladislav of Czechoslovakia from President Benes in 1938; and the Order of St. Sava from prince Paul of Yugoslavia in 1941.

Mr. Joukowsky has written the historical notes and has ar ranged these dances for the benefit of those who cannot ever hope to go to the far-off hills of Macedonia, Bulgaria or Greece.

Ann Paterson
PROFESSOR OF PHYSICAL EDUCATION
SAN FRANCISCO STATE COLLEGE

August, 1965.

vii

PREFACE

As more and more people become interested in travel and in international problems, they become interested, also, in the art, music and culture of other countries. Ethnic dance depicts as well as any medium the true spirit of a people. This book is intended to bring to the serious student of ethnic dance some insights into the customs of the people and some dances which he may otherwise never have known.

The emphasis throughout the book is from the simple dances to the more complicated ones. The book is not intended to be a book for beginners. It is for the person who already is converted to ethnic dance. One who has a purpose. For ethnic dance is like other forms of art. To be good, one must study, one must practice and practice and practice. He must be so familiar with the steps that they become part of him. The selection of the dances was done with the full knowledge that some are, indeed, very difficult. The reader should not become discouraged. Start with the simplest one and master it, then the more complex ones will be easy to learn.

Why have we decided to do this book? Why have we tried to bring dances together after so many long years of work? I have spent my entire life in the field of dance and from my earliest years I have paid attention to ethnic dance. Between the two wars in Europe when the State ensembles were reactivated, dances were done but they were found to be in very bad condition. Finding these dances so poorly done led me into the research which has taken me into many by-roads and brought me fascinating experiences. I have contact with most of Europe, and for many years each summer when the Balkan Theatre was not in session I devoted my time to digging out the ethnic treasures of the dance. Originally the idea was to bring together all these dances, the legends, stories, traditions, rhythms, melodies to start a new era in dance theater. As time went on and events took place making this impossible, I turned to sharing my collection at folk dance camps, schools and institutes. At the insistence of many good people this book has evolved.

The book is divided into ten sections. The first incorporates a definition of the term "ethnic" dance and gives the reader a few helpful hints about how to approach the teaching of ethnic dance. The next nine chapters include background information and dances from each of the following: Macedonia, Greece; Serbia; Bulgaria; Rumania; Czechoslovakia; Poland; Russia, Ukraine; and France.

The dances contain abbreviations which are well known to folk dancers. To aid the reader a list of abbreviations used appears at the end of the first chapter.

I wish to express my deep feeling first to the great country which adopted my little family and gave me the opportunity to find a place in the United States where I started over to make a second life. Second, I am very grateful to the family of colleagues who have helped me find new friends, and to participate in this important work of education. Third, I wish to thank Ann Paterson, San Francisco State College, without whose help this book would never have become a reality.

I am indebted to Ruth Ruling, distinguished research committee member of the University of the Pacific Folk Dance Camps who so graciously took notes from me when these dances were first introduced in the United States in Stockton, California.

The illustrations were drawn by Sergei Smirnoff and are authentic presentations of the costumes worn by dancers from each of the countries.

Further, I appreciate the many students who have offered me encouragement and help. For the careful typing of the manuscript I am grateful to Patricia J. Quance. Any errors or omissions are my responsibility alone.

Anatol M. Joukowsky
San Francisco

August, 1965

CONTENTS

THE
TEACHING
OF
ETHNIC DANCE

CHAPTER ONE

THE MEANING OF ETHNIC DANCE

For many centuries man has danced. Ethnic dance has been developed by the people. Ethnos in Greek means people. "Folk" is the Anglo-Saxon word meaning people, too. Basically, there is no difference in the real definitions of the two words, however, in the United States a slight variation in the meanings obtains and a discussion of this may serve to clarify the usage. Ethnic dance is one done by the people in the original place, in living form, today or yesterday. It is transferred or transported to a new place without any change and is performed as it was originally. The music is done without adaptation. Folk dance, as we use this term, describes a dance which initially was an ethnic dance but which has undergone some change through the years. It has gone from dancer to dancer, teacher to dancers, from a book to dancers and teachers and has been altered in the process of evolution. Like the museum piece, ethnic dance or fixed movement from the past of a people transfers the culture and knowledge of a people to present and future generations.

Ethnic Dance in Education

What does the term ethnic dance in education mean? One answer to this question may be found in the words of students in dance classes. Some of these students express themselves by stating that college curriculums are loaded with all kinds of requirements. They face many emotional problems. Dance is a natural outlet between classes, between long periods of sitting and working. Movement helps one free himself from his problems. Dance — all kinds of dance — provides a form of expres-

1

sion. Ethnic dance serves as a vehicle for understanding a different kind of life, gives a different meaning to life and a different point-of-view. Through ethnic dance one learns to appreciate how the people of another culture, another generation have lived. The ways of these countries may seem strange at first, but through understanding their dances one comes to an understanding then of the people. Through the rhythm which speaks through fascinating melodies of songs and the words of those songs one is not only a spectator but also a co-creator of the feeling of other people. This is ethnic dance. This is why the young American dancer who is busy with city life, with studies, busy with difficult life problems is so happy, so relaxed while doing ethnic dance.

It is not enough to know steps and patterns, one must know what type of dance one is doing and whence it comes. This is the most difficult task — but the most essential. Many are doing dances as if they were skeletons, just like a rock without meaning, without any significance. But ethnic dance starts to be dance only after one really knows, has understood the spirit of the country and what the steps mean. One can never dance a Bulgarian dance, for example, without being involved physically and spiritually in what one is doing. So, first, before one learns the patterns, before one meets the problems of this dance, before he develops the technique one should know what kind of spirit and feeling that dance represents.

If a person really is interested in performing ethnic dance with any authenticity, the author recommends reading carefully the notes about each country in this book and then studying the history, geography, and religious beliefs and everything he can find about the people from the places where these dances originate. Go to movies, talk with people from these lands, travel to see what can be found out. Then, perhaps, one can perform the dance as well as the people do in their own milieu. One cannot buy cheaply the experience of centuries.

Meaning of This Book for Teachers

This book is not an elementary folk dance book. This has been done ably by many others. It is an ethnic dance book which can be used by teachers especially trained in this kind of dance.

The most important thing for a good teacher of ethnic dance to achieve is the proper style and character of the dances. Patterns, steps, technique can be properly executed but yet the dance still looks wrong. Why is this? Because the feeling and the style are not right. How can one "catch" this spirit? This is very difficult to teach. For native dancers, of course, it is not hard because the feeling is natural, and they are only expressing their own backgrounds. But those who are not natives must get this from somewhere else.

The choice of good records is the key for discovering the right feeling of a dance. The selection of records at the beginning level is particularly important because dancers will establish the spirit and be able to carry this over into more difficult dances. Records are available in any large city, and if one lives in a small town he can obtain them from record houses by mail. (See page 6.)

Before any teaching begins, it is well to explain as much as possible the facts about the country, the beliefs, the customs and manners, the life of the people. Listening to music, songs or conversation is of importance.

Essential in teaching ethnic dance is the enthusiasm of the instructor for a dance. This comes from a thorough knowledge of any given dance and from a true love of dancing and teaching. It is not necessary, of course, to be a Serbian or a Rumanian to teach Serbian or Rumanian dances — but it *is* necessary to know how to transmit the information.

The serious teacher should use kinescopes or motion picture documentaries for visual exposition of the facts about the people or the dances one wishes to teach. Not only the motion pictures and documentaries about dances are important but anything which deals in an authentic way with the episodes in history will help. Books, stories, articles all are ways of becoming familiar with the soul of a nation.

Never stop learning, never think one knows enough. The material available is inexhaustible and could never be adequately covered by any one person. The exceptional teacher is the one who starts out perhaps not knowing too much, but who works, studies diligently taking advantage of every workshop, clinic, institute to become an expert and a leader. Nor is it necessary to become an expert in every country's dance. A teacher may become extremely interested in the dance of one particular country and concentrate on this yet know a little something about the other countries as well. For example, one could become well versed in Scandinavian or Slavic dances, yet know also the dances from Southeastern Europe or Latin America.

With a beginning class start with the simple dances. Choose dances appropriate to the group's ability. After the authentic record has been obtained listen many times to the music. Become familiar with the rhythm, the musical phrases, the repetitions and the structure of the music. The music is an integral part of the dance. The rhythmical accents are of great importance. In order to discover these correct accents, one needs time, understanding and concentration. The dance should not dominate the music nor should the music overshadow the dance. They go together. The records recommended here are the best available for accompaniment of these selected dances. Other music will not fit with the described steps.

After the teacher becomes familiar with the record the steps can then be put to the music. The group may have to practice the steps separately before they can put them into the pattern of the dance. Timing is exceedingly important so be certain to know the rhythm of the dance.

Be sure the dancers are prepared to meet the technical problems of the dance you expect to teach. Exercises and "warm-up" periods are appropriate and are recommended. Some leading ethnic schools like the Moiseyev Ethnic School have selected certain exercises which are proper for this preparation. Serious injury can result when the dancer is not properly prepared. Shin splints, torn muscles, turned ankles must be avoided and can be if a gradual program of preparation is followed.

The dances in this book go from simple to complicated. All present the ethnic steps of certain areas or districts and are adapted to the music (record) recommended with each dance. In several dances, two or three variations of the same step are presented. Each variation has certain principal ethnic elements. In order to learn the basic steps, repeat them many times. Start the movement slowly, be sure you are doing the step correctly, then build up a faster tempo ending in real speed. Do not expect miracles. It takes a long time to become expert in ethnic dance.

Keep in mind that all people will not be interested in becoming ethnic dancers. Some do not have any talent. But if one is basically enthusiastic he can learn and have great enjoyment through this kind of dance.

To summarize the admonitions:
1. Be in good health, be properly prepared by exercising.
2. Steep yourself in the history, culture of the people.
3. Take advantage of opportunities to see ethnic ensembles and folk ballet companies.
4. Be enthusiastic and know as much as possible.
5. Be willing to work hard.
6. Choose the proper music; listen to the music.
7. Practice steps slowly at first then faster and faster.
8. Start with simple dances and do these until they are perfected then go to more complicated ones.
9. Encourage all your students to travel, study, learn. Attend folk dance workshops, clinics, institutes.
10. Do not get discouraged.

ABBREVIATIONS USED IN DANCES

bkwd or bwd	backward
CCW	counter-clockwise
COH	Center of Hall
cpl	couple
ct or cts	count
ctr	center
CW	clockwise
diag	diagonal
dn	down
ft	foot
fwd	forward
H	hand
L	left
LOD	line of direction
M	man
meas	measure
opp	opposite
pos	position
ptr or ptnrs	partner
R	right
RLOD	reverse line of direction
sdwd or swd	sideward
twd	toward
W	woman
wt	weight

Sources For Records

All records used in this book may be obtained from:

Festival Records
   161 Turk Street
   San Francisco, California 94102

Folkcraft
   1159 Broad Street
   Newark, New Jersey 07114

Other music stores particularly ones dealing with ethnic records in cities may carry these records.

CHAPTER TWO

MACEDONIA AND GREECE

Macedonia is an old slavic country situated in the heart of the Balkan peninsula. It is divided into three parts: Macedonian republic in the Yugoslavian Federation; Greek Macedonia and Bulgarian Macedonia. It is a great country with living folklore. Rapid streams and rivers divide the high mountainous country into many smaller units. These villages are connected geographically along the rivers or the mountains and they have developed kindred traditions, including dances and costumes. Being members of one Macedonian family there is a thread of similarity, therefore, in their life, their approach to living and their occupations. All this gives special color to the songs and dances Macedonians perform. There are no more rich or important dance treasures than can be found in Macedonia. Long years ago travelling not by automobile, nor airplane, nor bus, but going by horseback, loaded heavily with all the things one needs for three months' existence in the wild mountains, we watched for these traditional dances to be performed. From one village to another we would try to arrive at the time of a big holiday or a marriage or some other important day in the village. We sat, watched how the people danced, then were invited to dance with the natives. How we enjoyed what they were doing, enjoyed what they were talking and thinking about. Always we looked for the underlying reasons for their traditions. This is the real way to understand the dance of Macedonia. All kinds of rhythms from 2/4 to 13/16 are to be found in Macedonia. These rhythms are part of the innate art of folk dance to the Mace-

donian. The Nevestinsko, Teshkoto, Lesnoto, any of the Macedonian dances call for special songs. The problem is from which
village will the rhythm come? It could be from Tetovo or from
Strumitza or maybe from Kavadar or Gevgeli. They are families, yes, but always just a little different. The "smell" is different, like the aroma from different blooming flowers of the
mountains.

There are enough Macedonian dances to keep one busy all
the rest of his life studying them. Many are forgotten. Those
that have survived are delightful representations of Macedonian
culture. To love the Macedonian dance one must go deeply inside the Macedonian life, watch the girls, the boys, ask them
questions, read about typical characteristics of the dances. Their

dances do not depict a realistic approach to life. They are spiritual, colorful, and suggest "I am a Macedonian, I am proud to be one." The dances reflect differing moments of life. For boys away from home in Paris, Istanbul or New York, doing the "Teshkoto" brings the far away Macedonian mountains close to home. The nostalgia engendered when three or four get together to dance with the beat of the tupans, the Macedonian drums is overwhelming. These people become transported back to their beloved mountains through their dances. Do not watch the steps, rather watch the body, the posture, the eyes.

In some speedy dances from the south such as from Prespa or from Ohrid-Lake or from Tikvech, one can get a glimpse of the dialogue of the mountain streams. Quick, short, slight steps like going from stone to stone down to the Aegean Sea. The fast dance far off in the south of Macedonia is the Chobansko. It means Shepherd's dance. It is the meditation on the philosophies of the mountains. It represents the thinking about the existence of mankind trying always to answer the "why," the eternal "why." They are not tragic dances. But they are religious. To many Macedonians, Christianity is an important factor in the attempt to answer questions.

The opening of the dance puts the question. They come to an understanding with their creator. One can see how close they are to the spirit *not* to mankind. The music is provided simply from a homemade creation of the shepherd. Find a record which presents the fine, clear sound made by this Macedonian ethnic instrument. Do not get one which is full of noises, made from many harmonicas or other sophisticated instruments.

The Macedonian dances presented here include "Lesnoto" meaning "easy dance." "Lesnoto" is one of the most primitive of the Macedonian dances. It is a kind of polonaise. In it, the people just walk and sing. Shy, young ladies from the village do the dance with featherlight steps. The legs are very highly ornamented, and so they are not lifted high in any Macedonian dance. The men dance with high, light, proud mountainous steps. In the beginning the dance is slow-moving like a moun-

tain cloud. Then in the end it goes into a cascade as if coming
from a mountain stream. The "Komitsko" is a dance done by
the heroes of the mountains. It depicts the resistance during the
Turkish occupation. The young braves are alone in the mountains and the dance is a description of resistance against all
enemies. The particular "Komitsko Oro" presented here has the
components of the Huma Village not far from Doiran Lake
where the three frontiers come together — Bulgaria, Macedonia,
Greece. Elements from all three countries can be seen in this
dance. These three countries were united long centuries fighting
against the common enemy, the Turks, until victory was won.
The dance is proud, full of suspicious movement, looking for
enemies. The victorious moments of the dance go into a trouble-
less happy dance.

Ergensko Oro is a very sophisticated dance and assumes a
complicated rhythm from 9 and 13/16th. For the dancer this is
no problem. He is not counting the score — he is dancing! The
rhythm is complicated because the old forgotten songs are like
this. The melody is a happy, light, gay one and builds in the
"oro" from slow to fast. The "Sto Mi Je Milo" dance is done
by young girls. The rhythm is 9/8ths and is an old wedding
dance from the Ohrid-Lake region.

In travelling in 1924, the author saw two or three versions of
this dance. The one presented here is an arrangement of all
three done by the author. "Sto Mi Je Milo" means How Happy
I Am. Sitting, looking through a little window watching the
beautiful girls from the village the dancer thinks how happy he
is. The girls gather water from the village fountain. This is an
important job for everyone but it is the special job of the un-
married girls to bring the mother of the house the water. The
dance starts in the morning, and the young ladies are still filling
their water jugs at the end of the day.

The "Staro Soadbarsko," an old wedding dance, again 9/8ths
meter, is a slow Turkish-type of dance movement. It shows the
influence of living and dancing under the Turks. The dance is
in open circle going around the bride. The bride is without

movement, heavily laden with beautiful clothes — ready for the wedding. This is the last dance of her friends before the next morning when she goes to the church to begin a new life. Sva Dba means "wedding." This dance has some strange movements which are mystical signs done by the hands. These bless the young lady who is leaving the company of her carefree, happy friends.

If the teacher of ethnic dance ever has a chance to travel to foreign parts, Macedonia is a country he will not wish to miss. Go to the small villages and stay for awhile. Get acquainted with the natives and learn from them. This will bring untold rewards to your dancing and teaching.

MACEDONIA
LESNOTO

SOURCE:	Learned in Southern Macedonia by Anatol Joukowsky. This Lesnoto has a 4 measure pattern instead of the usual 3.
MUSIC:	Record — Sperry 6115. 7/8 time. No introduction.
FORMATION:	Open circle. Hands joined and held shoulder height. When men dance alone hands are on adjacent shoulders. Start dance facing slightly left of LOD.
STEPS:	Take each step with a plié or bend of knee. As tempo accelerates steps become light jumps. The 7/8 meter used in this record consists of 3 accented beats divided as follows: 2/8, 2/8, 3/8.

PATTERN

Measures

1   2/8 Step R swd. to LOD.
       2/8 Wt. still on R, lift L across R.
       3/8 Step L in front of R.

2 2/8 Step R swd.

2/8 Wt. still on R start lifting L in front of R, knee bent. Body turns a little to R.

3/8 L knee arrives in pos. in front of R as R heel is raised and lowered.

3 Repeat action of Meas. 2, starting L.

2/8 + 2/8 Swing R ft. around behind L knee.

3/8 Step back R (1/8) close L to R (2/8).

Repeat above 4 meas. to end of record.

STO MI JE MILO
(How Much I Like This)

SOURCE: Dance from Ohrid-Lake District and learned by Anatol Joukowsky. In the Galicitza Region, the old version of this dance uses the older, slower steps. A more modern version is now danced throughout Yugoslavia, at a faster tempo.

MUSIC: Record — Sperry E3 KC 6135 Sto Me E Milo Em Drago. 9/8 time. No introduction.

FORMATION: Open circle or line. Hands joined and held shoulder ht. Line may have both M and W or there may be separate lines of M and W. M only dance their variation step when they are in a line without W. When M only are in a line the hand may be on upper arms of adjacent M.

STEPS: Every step is done with a plié or bend of knee. Wt. is on ball of ft. with heels close to floor. M lift ft. higher than W.

PATTERN

Measures

Complete pattern takes 2 meas. Begin facing slightly L of LOD.

1   Step R in LOD (ct. 1). Step L over R (ct. 2). Step R in LOD (ct. 3). Lift L knee still facing slightly L of LOD (ct. 4).

2   Face center L knee still lifted (ct. 1). Step L facing slightly R of R LOD (ct. 2). Touch R in front of L, toe out (ct. 3). Lift R knee and turn to face slightly L of LOD (ct. 4).

Men's Solo Version

During vocal follow pattern above omitting touch in meas. 2. Instead, R knee is lifted, toe turned out. When there is no vocal use pattern below.

1   Step R in LOD (ct. 1). Step L over R (ct. 2). Step R in LOD (ct. 3). Lift L knee still facing slightly L of LOD (ct. 4).

2   Face center L knee still lifted (ct. 1). Step L facing slightly R of R LOD (ct. 2). Jump into knee bend (see note) (ct. 3). Recover to standing pos. wt. still on L (ct. 4).

Note: On jump land facing slightly R of RLOD. Wt. predominantly on L. R knee slightly ahead of L. Back is straight.

STARO SVADBARSKO
(Old Wedding Dance)

SOURCE: Dance done in the Skopsko area of Macedonia and learned there by Anatol Joukowsky. It is an old dance performed by girls around the bride on the eve of her wedding.

MUSIC: Record — XOPO (Horo) X305-A Skopsko Horo. 7/8 time. No introduction.

FORMATION: Open circle or line. Hands are joined by interlocking last two fingers of right hand through last two fingers of neighbor.

STEPS: Knees are flexible and steps are not too large. Because of the 7/8 time (3/8, 2/8, 2/8) the steps are
described below showing the relationship between
the count and the step.

Figure I — 8 meas. done facing center.

Meas. 1 — Step R (ct. 1). Close L to R (cts. 2,3).

Meas. 2 — Step L (ct. 1). Close R to L (cts. 2,3).

Meas. 3 — Step R (ct. 1). Cross L behind R (no
wt.) (cts. 2,3).

Meas. 4 — Step L (ct. 1). Cross R behind L (no
wt.) (cts. 2,3).

Meas. 5 — Step R (ct. 1). Step L behind R (ct. 2).
Step R in place (ct. 3).

Meas. 6 — Step L (ct. 1). Step R behind L (ct. 2).
Step L in place (ct. 3).

Meas. 7 — Step R fwd. with lift of L knee (cts. 1,2).
Step fwd. L (ct. 3).

Meas. 8 — Step back R in place (ct. 1). Close L to
R (cts. 2,3).

Figure II — 2 meas. done in LOD.

Meas. 1 — Step fwd. R and lift L heel out (ct. 1).
Step L in LOD (ct. 2). Step R in LOD (ct. 3).

Meas. 2 — Step L in LOD (ct. 1). Bring R around
in front of L and close to L. Toes out (cts. 2,3).

Figure III — 2 meas. Moves LOD. Hips follow ft.
but shoulders face twds. center.

Meas. 1 — Step R in LOD (ct. 1). Step L in LOD
(ct. 2). Step R in LOD (ct. 3).

Meas. 2 — Step L in LOD turn toe to ctr. (ct. 1).
Close R to L (no wt.) (face ctr.) (cts. 2,3).

PATTERN

Measures

Figure I

1-32   Face center. Dance Fig I, 4 times.

Arms: hands are joined and down at start of dance. On meas. 1-2 they are raised to shoulder level. They stay there meas. 3-6. On meas. 7-8 they are brought up, out and back down to sides (hands still joined). They inscribe part of a CW circle.

Figure II

1-8   Turn to face LOD. Hands are joined and down. Dance Fig. II 4 times.

Figure III

1-16   Dance Figure I two times.

Figure IV

1-6   Dance Fig. II three times.

7-8   With same step and styling, turn R once around. Drop hands on turn and rejoin on completion.

9-16   Repeat all once more.

Figure V

1-12   Dance Fig. I two times.

Figure VI

1-16   Arms raised to shoulder height. Dance Fig. III 8 times.

Figure VII

1-16   Dance Fig. I two times.

Figure VIII

1-16   Dance Fig. III 8 times.

Figure IX

1-8   Dance Fig. I once and end with bow to center.

KOMITSKO ORO
(Resistance Dance)

SOURCE: Learned in Huma, Macedonia by Anatol Joukowsky. Komitsko Oro imitates in its movements the
activities of the Komita who were people that re-
sisted domination by Turks. Since the area in
which this dance was done was near the borders of
Macedonia, Greece and Bulgaria the steps have
the styling of these three countries.

MUSIC: Record — Newtone M-7 Aide Pushka Pukna. 2/4
time. 10 measure introduction. Dance begins with
first vocal.

FORMATION: Open kolo (broken circle). Hands on neighbor's
shoulders with right arm in front of neighbor's
left arm. Face a little left of Line of Direction
(LOD).

PATTERN

Measures

10 Meas. Introduction.

Figure I

10 Meas. Each step is done on one beat of music but because
of the pattern it is much easier to disregard the meas.
and consider just 20 cts. which is broken into groups
of 7, 7 and 6.
Step R in LOD (ct. 1). Step 1 in LOD (ct. 2). Facing
ctr., step R to R side (ct. 3). Lift bent L leg, knee
turned out, in front of R (ct. 4). Step L to L side
(ct. 5). Lift bent R leg, knee turned out, in front of
L (ct. 6). Step R beside L and prepare to repeat
whole pattern moving to L with L (ct. 7). On cts. 1-3
slowly raise R hand to just above the eyes as if shield-
ing them from the sun. Look to R and keep hand in
pos. for cts. 4-6. Return to place on ct. 7.

Repeat action of cts. 1-7 but moving to L with L and raising L hand (cts. 8-14).

Repeat action of cts. 1-7, moving to R with R but omit last step on R (cts. 15-20). This leaves R leg lifted in front of L.

Figure II

1   Hands are brought down and joined with neighbor. Hop on L, with R knee lifted high (ct. 1). Step R (ct. &). Hop on R, with L knee lifted high (ct. 2). Step L (ct. &). While doing above pattern travel in LOD.

2   Run R, L, R, L in LOD.

3-8   Repeat action of meas. 1-2 three more times (4 in all). On meas. 8 run only R (ct. 1), L (ct. &). Step R next to L (ct. 2). Hold (ct. &). End facing ctr.

Figure III

1   Clasp hands behind back at waist level. Assume slight crouch. Moving into ctr., step R in front of and a little to L of L ft. (ct. 1). Bend R (ct. &). Step L in front of and a little to R of R ft. (ct. 2). Bend L (ct. &).

2   Straightening body, step R and at same time extend L ft. fwd. and low (ct. 1). Bend L leg so L ft. is to R of R knee (ct. &). Return L to ct. 1 pos. (ct. 2). Bend L leg so L ft. is to L side of R knee (ct. &). All movements in meas. 2 have a staccato quality.

3   Moving out of circle, step back on L (ct. 1). Bend L (ct. &). Step back on R (ct. 2). Bend R (ct. &).

4   Step back on L (ct. 1). Step back on R (ct. &). Step L next to R (ct. 2). Hold (ct. &).

5-8   Repeat action of meas. 1-4.
Dance is repeated from beginning 4 more times.

ERGENSKO ORO
(Unmarried Boys' Dance)

SOURCE: This is a man's dance from the Ohrid-Lake region of Macedonia. It was learned by Anatol Joukowsky in Ohrid in 1932 and was adapted by him to fit the music of S. Hristic, "The Legend of Ohrid Lake."

MUSIC: Record — Jugoton LPY 25.
           This oro is in 9/16 and 13/16 alternating 1 meas. of each. This 9/16 meter consists of 2/16, 3/16, 2/16, 2/16 so that 4 beats are felt with no 2 being longer. The 13/16 meter consists of 2/16, 3/16, 2/16, 2/16, 2/16, 2/16 so that 6 beats are felt with no. 2 again being the longer. The measure will be written in counts with count 2 being underlined to note that it is of longer duration. The Introduc-

tion only has 3 measures consisting of 9/16, 13/16, 11/16. This will be written with count 2 being underlined.

FORMATION: Dancers in a broken circle with hands joined and held shoulder height. The right hand supports the left hand of the dancer to the right.

STEPS: *Basic Step I (9/16)*: Step R to R side (ct. 1). Step L across in front of R *(ct. 2)*. Step R to R side (ct. 3). Step L across behind R (ct. 4).
Basic Step II (13/16): Step R to R side (ct. 1). Hop on R, starting to cross L over R *(ct. 2)*. Step L in front of R (ct. 3). Step R to R side (ct. 4). Step L in front of R (ct. 5). Hop on L, placing R ft. behind L leg (ct. 6).

PATTERN

Measures

3 meas. Stand in place. This is a meas. each of 9/16, 13/16, and 11/16. Count (to yourself), 1, 2, 3, 4 - 1, 2, 3, 4, 5, 6 - 1, 2, 3, 4, 5.

1 (9/16) Facing a little L of LOD, dance Basic Step I, moving in LOD.

2 (13/16) Continuing, dance Basic Step II.

3-8 Repeat action of meas. 1-2 three times.

9-10 Turning to face ctr., dance one Basic Step I and one Basic Step II twd. ctr.

11-12 Moving away from ctr. (back up), dance one Basic Step I and one Basic Step II.
Repeat these 12 meas. of dance until the end of the music.

KUTZOVLASHKO (MAKEDONSKO ORO)
(Macedonian Tribal Dance)

SOURCE: Noted by Anatol Joukowsky in Mt. Karadjitza, Macedonian Highlands, 1936. The dance is from the Macedonian tribe, Karakatchani, of nomad shepherds. As these shepherds originally lived in Rumania, the character of the dance is Rumanian.

MUSIC: Record—"Kutzovlashko Oro," Sperry, E3 KB 6114.

FORMATION: For as many as wish to dance: a line of men, hands joined at shoulder height, elbows bent; facing a line of women, hands joined at sides. *Note:* There may be extra men at right end of men's line, or extra women at left end of women's line. Lines should start at least six feet apart.

STEPS: 1. *Active:* 4/8 and 6/8 time — 10 cts.
             Meas. 1 (4/8, 4 cts.) — step R ft. to R (ct. 1); hop on R ft. as L ft., L knee bent, is brought across in front of R ft. (ct. 2); step on L ft., crossed in front of R ft. (ct. 3); bend L knee, holding R ft. off floor (ct. 4).
             Meas. 2 (6/8, 6 cts.) — five small steps backwards, R,L,R,L,R, hold, wt. on R ft.
             Repeat these two meas. (10 cts.) to L, starting: step L ft. to L (ct. 1); etc. Repeat these 4 meas. (20 cts.)
             2. *Passive:* 4/8 and 6/8 time — 10 cts.
             Meas. 1 (4/8, 4 cts.) — step R ft. to R (ct. 1); bend R knee (ct. 2); step L ft. across in back of R ft. (ct. 3); bend both knees, keeping wt. on L ft. (ct. 4).
             Meas. 2 (6/8, 6 cts.) — step R ft. to R; step L ft. next to R ft.; step R ft. to R; step L ft. next to R ft.; step R ft. to R; bend R knee, keeping wt. on R ft. Repeat these two meas. (10 cts.) to L,

starting: step L ft. to L, etc. Repeat these 4
meas. (20 cts.).

3. *Cross-Step-Hop-Step:* 4/8 time — 4 cts.
   Step R ft. across in front of L ft. (ct. 1); Step L
   ft. in place, lifting R ft., knee bent (ct. 2); hop
   on L ft. (ct. 3); step R ft. to R (ct. 4). Repeat
   these 4 cts. starting: step L ft. across in front of
   R ft. (ct. 1); etc.

4. *Progressive Step* (sideward run): 4/8 time.
   Moving CCW around room.
   M's step: step R ft. across in front of L ft. (ct.
   1); step L ft. to L (ct. 2); repeat action cts. 1-2
   (cts. 3-4); repeat run as dance requires.
   W's step: step R ft. to R (ct. 1); step L ft. across
   behind R ft. (ct. 2); repeat action cts. 1-2 (cts.
   3-4); repeat run as dance requires.

PATTERN

Measures

A. (4/8 &
6/8 time)

Figure I

1-8   M's hands joined at shoulder level as in FORMA-
       TION.
       W's hands joined at sides as in FORMATION.
       M perform *active* step 4 times: R, 10 cts.: L 10 cts.:
       R 10 cts.; L 10 cts.; at same time the W perform
       Passive step 4 times: R 10 cts.; L 10 cts.; R 10 cts.;
       L 10 cts.

extra cts.

1 & 2   M lower joined hands; W raise joined hands, elbows
        bent.

Figure II

1-8   M perform *passive* step 4 times, R, L, R, L (40 cts.);
       while the W perform *active* step 4 times, R, L, R, L
       (40 cts.).

Figure III

1-8   Hands held as in Pattern II; M perform *active* step 4 times, R, L, R, L (40 cts.); while W perform *passive* step 4 times, R, L, R, L.

extra cts.

1 & 2   M raise joined hands, elbows bent; W lower joined hands.

Figure IV Women's Turn

1-8   M perform *passive* step 4 times, R, L, R, L (40 cts.), while W perform *active* step with variation as described: W step R ft. to R (ct. 1); hop on R ft. as L ft., L knee, bent, is brought across in front of R ft. (ct. 2); step on L ft., crossed in front of R ft. (ct. 3); bend L knee, holding R ft. off floor (ct. 4); with hands outstretched, turn CW in individual circle, one complete turn with 5 small steps (R, L, R, L, R); hold wt. on R ft. and rejoin hands (ct. 10). Repeat the action of these 10 cts. starting to L (10 cts.); repeat all (20 cts.).

extra cts.

1 & 2   M lower joined hands; W raise joined hands, elbows bent.

Figure V Men's Turn

1-8   M perform *active* step with variation, as described for W, Fig. IV (40 cts.); while W performs *passive* step 4 times, R, L, R, L.

Figure VI. M & W Active with M's Variation

1-8   M perform *active* step with variation as described: M step R ft. to R (ct. 1); hop on R ft. as L ft., L knee bent, is brought across in front of R. ft. (ct. 2); step on L ft., crossed in front of R ft. (ct. 3); bend L knee, and at same time, tap R toe behind L ft. (ct. 4); step 5 small steps backwards, R, L, R, L, R; (cts. 5, 6, 7, 8, 9); hold, wt. on R ft. (ct. 10). Repeat action of these 10 cts. to L (10 cts.). Repeat all 20 cts. W perform *active* step, without any variation 4 times, R, L, R, L.

extra cts.

1-10   M's and W's lines move twd. each other with 10 small running steps. On 10th ct., M join R hand with R hand of opposite W; join L hand with L hand of next W. M at L end of M's line places his L hand on hip. This position of hands is kept throughout remainder of dance.

B. (4/8 time)

Figure VII. Cross-Step-Hop-Step 4/8 time

1-8   M and W both perform Step No. 3, both starting step R ft. across L, alternating step pattern, R, L, R, L, R, L, R, L 8 times in all (32 cts.).

Figure VIII. Progression (sideward run) 4/8 time

1-9   Both M and W perform Step No. 4, moving joined lines CCW around room (36 cts.).

Figure IX. Cross-Step-Hop-Step

1-8   Repeat action of Fig. VII (32 cts.).

Figure X. Progression (sideward run)

1-6   Perform Step No. 4, moving joined lines CCW around room (24 cts.).

Figure XI. Cross-Step-Hop-Step

1-8   Repeat action Fig. VII (32 cts.).

Figure XII. Progression (sideward run)

1-7   Perform Step No. 4, moving joined lines CCW around room (28 cts.).

Finish

2 chords   Bow, first to R person, then to L person.

As we have already pointed out, Greece and Macedonia are very closely connected. So this Greek dance is presented along with the Macedonian ones.

Because there are so many Greek dances and books about Greek dances the author has included only one dance here. One dance "Gerakina" is performed all over Greece. Its meaning comes from a lovely legend. In 1924 going from Sparta through the mountains to the Kalamata we stopped at a little village. It is no longer on the map. She probably changed her Slavic name Zarnitza to a more Hellenic one. We passed an open store. Very like a general store in the United States. They sold everything. We went into the store and started to talk with the owner and his wife. We talked and talked and finally ended with coffee. We talked only of dances. The wife was from the Macedonian mountains of Greece and she showed us this dance, Gerakina. The song was from the little town of Trikala. Gerakina came to take the cold water from the fountain and fell into the cistern. She started to make a noise and then everyone in the village came and huddled around, but no one would jump into the cold water to rescue her. Except one young man. He made this proposition. "I will save you Gerakina from this cold situation if you will marry me." Having no other alternative available, she accepted him. She took ahold of his golden belt (the sign for a good, new life) and he saved her. The dance is a Kalamatiano sirto (Gerakina — from Peloponesseus). The movements of this dance go along with the expression of the song. One can easily see the whole story unfolding. This dance is in 7/8ths time. The patterns in new versions are quite different from the dance described here.

GREECE
GERAKINA
(Gair′ ah kee na)
(Girl's Name)

SOURCE: Learned in Greece by Anatol Joukowsky, 1925, Zarnitza (Peloponez).

MUSIC: Records — Folkways FP 814 Side I, band 3. Victor 26-822 OB. Liberty 84A.

FORMATION: Open circle. Dancers join hands with L arm extended diag. L, about shoulder height; R arm with elbow bent, shoulder high; R forearm horizontal beneath and supporting extended L arm of next dancer. Dancers face diag. R and circle moves to R (CCW).

Gerakina is in 7/8 meter, counted 1-2-3, 1-2, 1-2. This may also be stated 3/8, 2/8, 2/8. Sometimes the 2/8, 2/8 is combined to give a step 4/8 in duration. In the cts. given below ct. 1 is always 3/8, ct. 2 is 4/8. If the meas. has cts. 1, 2, and ct. 1 is 3/8, ct. 2 is 2/8 and ct. & is also 2/8. This dance starts out quiet and restrained, no hop in the first figure, not much distance covered. On each repeat there is more vigor and momentum for the M. W remain feminine; they do not hop, merely lift on the toe, but they do make a strong sweep with the L leg on ct. 2 of the last meas. Turns are sharp. Eyes are low during Fig. II. The knees turn, not the hips on the Droom steps.

STEPS: *Walk:* short and springy with a relaxed knee.
Touch: always done with R ft. May be done once, twice or 4 times. Wt. on L, touch ball of R ft. in front of, and close to toe of L. R heel close to floor. R toe may point in (to L) or out (to R).

Short Droom: Step L (ct. 1). Touch R, toe in (ct. 2). Touch R, toe out (ct. &).

Long Droom and Pose: (2 meas.) Wt. is already on L. Touch R 4 times: toe in (ct. 1). Toe out (ct. 2). Toe in (ct. &). Toe out (ct. 1). Strike following pose on ct. 2. Release hands. Leave L arm extended diag. palm of hand toward center with fingers pointing up. R arm behind back, palm out. Lift R leg, knee bent, heel held in front of L knee.

PATTERN

Measures

cts. 2 &   Introduction

1   *Figure I. Grapevine*
              Step R in LOD (ct. 1). Hop R and start moving L (upbeat). Step L in front of R (ct. 2). Step R in LOD, turning to face ctr. (ct. &). S (hop) QQ
              Note: Hop after ct. 1 is omitted the 1st time through but is done in all the repeats.

2   Step L bk. of R (ct. 1). Touch R, toe out (ct. 2).   SS

3-8   Repeat action of meas. 1-2 three times (4 in all).

              Figure II. Forward and Short Droom
              Keeping hands joined, drop arms down. Face LOD (CCW).

9   Step R (ct. 1.). Step L (ct. 2). Step R (ct. &).   SQQ

10   Short Droom as described above.   SQQ

11   Step R (ct. 1). Step L (ct. 2). Step R (ct. &).   SQQ

12   Step L, turning to face ctr. (ct. 1). Raise joined hands fwd. Touch R twd. ctr. (ct. 2).   SS

              Figure III. To the center and Drop Back
13-14   Moving fwd. twd. ctr. of circle, repeat action of Fig. II meas. 9-10.   SQQ SQQ

15   Moving bkwd. away from ctr., drop back into sitting
        position on R ft., L toe touching floor in front of R,
        then flicking fwd. with slight kick (ct. 1). Step bkwd.
        L (ct. 2). Step bkwd. R (ct. &).   SQQ

16   Repeat action of meas. 15, starting L.

        Figure IV. Long Droom, Pose and Solo Turn
17-18   Long Droom and pose as described in steps above

                                                          SQQ SS

19   Without changing arms, each dancer turns CW in
        place. Step R (ct. 1), L (ct. 2), R (ct. &). End facing
        ctr.   SQQ

20   Step L (ct. 1). Touch R (ct. 2).
        Repeat entire dance to end of record.
        Note: This version of Gerakina is the old Greek-
        Macedonian dance unadulterated by the process of
        evolution. The versions done today are very differ-
        ent from this one.

CHAPTER THREE

SERBIA

The State of Serbia is a basic part of the Yugoslav Federation. The Serbs call themselves SRBI and are a Slavonic people. They have the same origins and language as the Croats. But the Croats use the Latin alphabet while the Serbs use the Cyrillic alphabet (the same as the Russians use).

The Serbian people, like so many others, have been the target of many invasions. The Turkish invasion being one of the most devastating. This gallant State has a long history of struggle for independence and resistance to all these occupations through the centuries. This is clearly reflected in the Serbian dances. The proud dignity, full posture of the Serbian dancer is warrior-like in style. The Kolo, a round formation dance has endless local forms depending upon the place from where it came. So, too, with the costumes which vary from village to village. These are all beautifully embroidered hand-made tissues, and reflect the affection which Serbian women have toward their dances. The women wear their hair in a style close to vizantic (using the hair to make crowns of braids around the top of the head). The Serbs wear special moccasin-like shoes called opanke.

For every significant occasion the Kolos are the most representative of the expression of the Serbian spirit. Between the two world wars, the Serbian Society adopted the tradition of starting all their big balls with the Kolo. If the King were present they would begin with the Kraljevo Kolo (the King's Kolo), if he were not the dignitaries who were present would start by leading with a Serbianka (Serbian Girl) or a Kolo dedicated to the special sponsor of the ball.

The Kolos presented in this book are samples of the old dances, some versions are arranged in medley form.

SELJANCICA
(Sell yahn chee tsa)

SOURCE: Learned in Serbia by Anatol Joukowsky. This is one of the most popular of the kolos. Also called "Student's Kolo."

MUSIC: Record — Jogoton C6259 recommended because tempo increases during dance. 2/4 meter.

FORMATION: Open kolo (broken circle). Hands are joined and held down. Leader at R and person at other end of line place free hand in a fist behind back. All face center.

STEPS: All steps are done with plié or bend of knee. The tempo of this kolo increases as dance progresses. The steps do not change basically but there is an adjustment necessary to enable the dancer to keep up with the music. There should be a gradual change from the steps danced to the slower music to the steps used with the faster music.

PATTERN

Measures

SLOW TEMPO
Figure I. Side Step

A 1   Step R to R (ct. 1). Close L to R (ct. 2).

   2   Step R to R (ct. 1). Close L to R (no wt.) (ct. 2).

   3-4 Repeat action of meas. 1-2 starting L to L.

   5-8 Repeat action of meas. 1-4.

Figure II. Step, Close

B 9   Step R to R (ct. 1). Close L to R (no wt.) (ct. 2).

   10   Step L to L (ct. 1). Close R to L (no wt.) (ct. 2).

11-12   Repeat action of meas. 9-10.

Figure III. Walking

C 13-15   Turning to Face LOD (CCW), walk 6 steps starting R (1 to a ct.).

16   Step R in LOD but turn to face ctr. (ct. 1). Close L to R (no wt.) (ct. 2). On closing step turn to face RLOD (CW).

17-19   In RLOD walk 6 steps starting L.

20   Step L in RLOD but turn to face ctr. (ct. 1). Close L to R (no wt.) (ct. 2). End facing ctr.

Continue the above pattern until the tempo calls for the gradual change to following pattern.

MEDIUM TEMPO

Figure I. Side Step

A 1   Step R to R (ct. 1). Step L behind R (ct. 2).

2   Step R to R (ct. 1). Touch L in front of R (ct. 2).

3-4   Repeat action of meas. 1-2 starting to L with L.

5-8   Repeat action of meas. 1-4.

Figure II. Step, Touch

B 9   Step R (ct. 1). Touch L in front of R (ct. 2).

10   Step L (ct. 1). Touch R in front of L (ct. 2).

11-12   Repeat action of meas. 9-10.

Figure III. Walking

C 13-20   Use same walking pattern as in Figure III (Slow Tempo). Steps may be shorter because of increasing tempo.

Continue the above pattern until the tempo calls for the gradual change to the following pattern.

FAST TEMPO

Figure I. Side Step

A 1   Step R to R (ct. 1). Step L behind R (ct. 2).

2   Step R to R (ct. 1). Lift L leg (knee bent) in front of R (ct. 2). R heel lifts as L leg crosses in front of R.

3-4   Repeat action of meas. 1-2 starting to L.

5-8   Repeat action of meas. 1-4.

Figure II. Step, Swing

B 9   Step R (ct. 1). Lift L leg (knee bent) in front of R (ct. 2). R heel lifts as L leg crosses.

10   Repeat action of meas. 9 starting to L.

11-12   Repeat action of meas. 9-10.

Figure III. Running

C 13-20   Use same pattern as Figure III (Slow Tempo) but running steps are used instead of walking steps. Continue above pattern until end of music.

KOLO FROM SUMADIJA
(Round Dance)

SOURCE: Kolo from Sumadija (Shu mah dee yah) was learned by Anatol Joukowsky from the natives in Yugoslavia.

MUSIC: Record — Sonart M-212B Shumadiya Kolo. 2/4 time. No introduction.

FORMATION: Lines of 6 people. Hold onto belts of neighbors with L arm in front of neighbor's R arm. End dancers place free hand behind back. Separate into groups of 4 lines. Each group of 4 lines arrange themselves to form a square, facing in.

STEPS: Knees are flexible. Each step is done with a plié or bend of knee.
Heel Lift: This is a hop that has been diminished to the point where only the heel leaves the ground.
Weaving Run: One step to a count. On each running step forward cross the stepping foot in front

of weight-bearing foot. When going backward, cross the stepping foot behind the weight-bearing foot. This gives a "weaving effect."

PATTERN

Measures

Figure I. Side-Step

1   Step to R side with R (ct. 1). Cross L behind R (ct. 2).

2   Step to R side with R (ct. 1). Heel lift on R as L leg (knee bent) is lifted in front of R lower leg (ct. 2).

3-4   Repeat action of meas. 1-2 but start to L with L.

5-16   Repeat action of meas. 1-4 three times (8 side-steps

Figure II. Long Side Step

1   Step to R side with R (ct. 1). Cross L behind R (ct. 2).

2-3   Repeat action of meas. 1 (Fig. II) two times.

4   Step to R side with R (ct. 1). Heel lift on R and L leg (knee bent) is lifted in front of R lower leg (ct. 2).

5-8   Repeat action of meas. 1-4 (Fig. II) but start to L with L.

9-16   Repeat action of meas. 1-8 (Fig. II).

Figure III. Cross Step

1   Step R across in front of L with accent (ct. 1). Body is slightly bent fwd. over R. L ft. remains in place. Step back on L in place (ct. 2).

2   Step R next to L (ct. 1). Step L in place (ct. &). Step R in place (ct. 2). Hold (ct. &).

3-4   Repeat action of meas. 1-2 (Fig. III) but start with L across in front of R.

5-16   Repeat action of meas. 1-4 (Fig. III) 3 times (8 Cross

Steps in all). On meas. 16, last ct. &, do not hold but instead step R in preparation for Fig. IV.

Figure IV. Back and Forward

1   Step on L directly behind R heel (ct. 1). Small hop on L as R leg is brought in arc around behind L (ct. &). Step on R directly behind L heel (ct. 2). Small hop on R as L leg is brought in arc around behind R (ct. &). There will be a small amount of movement backward during this meas.

2   Step L behind R heel (ct. 1). Small step fwd. on R (ct. &). Close L up to R heel (ct. 2). Small step fwd. on R (ct. &). This meas. should produce movement fwd. to balance bkwd. movement of meas. 1 (Fig. III).

3-16   Repeat action of meas. 1-2 (Fig. III) 7 times (8 in all). Step always starts with L. On meas. 16 hold last ct. &.

Interlude

1-8   Turning a little to R, walk 7 small steps along side of the imaginary square. Beg. R and ct. 2 of meas. 4. Keep lines straight. Turning a little to L, walk 7 steps back to place. Beg. L and hold ct. 2 of meas. 8.

1-16   Repeat action of Fig. I.

1-16   Repeat action of Fig. II.

1-16   Repeat action of Fig. III.

Figure V. Heel Bounce

1   Feet together. Swing heels to R, raising and lowering heels 3 times (cts. 1, &, 2). Hold ct. &. This would be 3 small bounces.

2   Repeat action of meas. 1 (Fig. V) but swing heels to L.

3   With larger movement, bounce heels once to R (ct. 1). Do 1 large bounce to L (ct. 2).

4   In ctr., do 3 small heel bounces (cts. 1, &, 2).

5-16   Repeat action of meas. 1-4 (Fig. V) 3 times (4 patterns in all).

Figure VI. Weaving Run

1-2   With body bent fwd., do 4 weaving run steps fwd. beg. R.

3-4   Straightening body, do 4 weaving run steps back to place beg. R.

5-16   Repeat action of meas. 1-4 (Fig. VI) 3 times (in and out 4 times in all).

1-16   Repeat action of Fig. I.

1-12   Repeat action of Fig. II. Music fades out so Fig. II is not completed.

AJDE JANO
(Ai deh Yah no)
(Let's Go)

SOURCE: Ajde Jano is a dance from Kosmet, a region of southern Serbia.

MUSIC: Record — Jugoton C6447. 4 measure Introduction.

FORMATION: Open Kolo (broken circle). Hands joined and held down. Face in LOD (CCW).

STEPS: Every step is done with a plié or bend of knee. Weight is on balls of feet with heels close to ground.
             Ajde Jano is in 7/8 meter, consisting of 3/8, 2/8, 2/8, so that 3 beats are felt in each measure, the first being the longest. Sometimes the 2/8, 2/8,

part of the measure is combined to give a step of 4/8 duration. Dance pattern takes 5 measures to complete but the melody is in 8 or 12 measures phrase.

PATTERN

Count

Introduction: 4 measures. Stand in place.
Measure I

3/8   Step R in LOD.

4/8   Step L in LOD. Toe turned out a little to L.

Measure II

3/8   Step R in LOD.

2/8   Step L in LOD.

2/8   Step R in LOD.

Measure III

3/8   Step L twd. ctr. and face ctr.

4/8   Lift L heel and raise R leg (knee bent) in front of L.

Measure IV

3/8   Step R in front of L.

4/8   Touch L fwd., toe turned out to L. R knee bends.

Measure V

3/8   Step bkwd. L (out of circle).

2/8   Step bkwd. R.

2/8   Step L next to R.

Repeat meas. 1-5 to end of music.

Note: When movement is in to ctr. (meas. 3, 4) hands are slowly raised (no higher than eye level). On meas. 5, hands are lowered to beginning position.

ZABARKA
(Zah' bar kah)
(Frog Dance)

SOURCE: Zabarka was learned in Yugoslavia by Anatol Joukowsky.

MUSIC: Record — Jugoton C6210. No introduction.

FORMATION: Open kolo (broken circle). Hands joined and down. Face in LOD (CCW).

STEPS: Every step is done with a plié or bend of knee. Weight is on balls of feet with heels close to floor. Zabarka is in 4/4 meter. This orchestration is in modern Yugoslavian style as it uses four guitars instead of traditional instruments.

PATTERN

Measures

Figure I

1　Step R in LOD (cts. 1-2). Step L in LOD (cts. 3-4).

2　Repeat action of meas. 1.

3　Step R in LOD (cts. 1-2). Touch L in LOD, toe turned twd. ctr. of circle (cts. 3-4).

4　Step bkwd. L, diag. R of RLOD (ct. 1). Step bkwd. R, diag. R of RLOD (ct. 2). Step L next to R (ct. 3). Hold (ct. 4).

5-16　Repeat action of meas. 1-4 three times (4 in all).

Figure II

1　Face ctr., progress slightly to R. Step R (cts. 1-2). Hop R (ct. 3). Step L in front of R (ct. 4).

2　Step R (cts. 1-2). Hop R (ct. 3). Step L in bk. of R (ct. 4).

3　Repeat action of meas. 1.

4   Step R bending R knee (cts. 1-2). Step L next to R (ct. 3). Step R in place (ct. 4).

5-8   Repeat action of meas. 1-4, starting L and progressing slightly to L.

Figure III

1   Facing ctr., small step R to R (ct. 1). Bend R knee and bring L ft. in front of R so L heel is over R instep (ct. 2). Straightening R knee, lift R heel and bring L ft. around behind R (ct. 3). Step L behind R (ct. 4). During step knees are close together and L ft. is close to R leg.

2   Step to R with R (ct. 1). Step L behind R (ct. 2). Step R to R (ct. 3). Step L behind R (ct. 4).

3-6   Repeat action of meas. 1-2 twice.

7   Repeat action of meas. 1.

8   Step R to R (ct. 1). Step L behind R (ct. 2). Step R to R (ct. 2). Hold (ct. 4).

9-16   Repeat action of meas. 1-8, starting L and moving L.

Figure IV

1-3   Repeat action of Fig. III meas. 1, three times.

4   Step R bending knee (cts. 1-2). Step L next to R (ct. 3). Step R in place (ct. 4).

5-8   Repeat action of meas. 1-4, starting with L to L.

9-16   Repeat action of meas. 1-8.

Figure I (repeated)

1-8   Repeat action of Fig. I meas. 1-4 twice. Omit hold on ct. 4 of meas. 8.

Figure V

1   Facing ctr., reach to R side with R and step on it (ct. 4 of meas. before). Close L to R (ct. 1). Reach to R with R (ct. 2). Close L to R (ct. 3). Reach to R with R (ct. 4).

2   Close L to R (ct. 1). In place, leap onto R (ct. 2). Step
          L next to R (ct. &). Stamp R in place (no wt.) (ct. 3).
          Reach to R with R (ct. 4).

3-16   Repeat action of meas. 1-2 seven times (8 in all). On
          meas. 16, hold ct. 4. Repeat whole dance from be-
          ginning with one exception. After Fig. IV is done,
          go directly into Fig. V. Omit the repeat of Fig. I.

          Note: In order to go from Fig. IV to Fig. V, an ad-
          justment must be made. In Fig. IV meas. 16: step L,
          bending knee (cts. 1-2). Hold ct. 3. Reach to R with
          R (start of Fig. V) (ct. 4).

STARA DUNDA

SOURCE: Learned and danced in Yugoslavia by Anatol
              Joukowsky.

MUSIC: Record — Pesme i Igre Narodna Jugoslavije, Ra-
              dio-Televizija Beograd LP 103. 2/4 meter.

FORMATION: Dancers in open circle, facing ctr., leader at R
              end. Hands joined and held down.

STEPS: *Dunda Step:* (1 step to a meas.) Hop on L (ct. 1).
              Small Step to R on R (ct. &). Step L next to R (ct.
              2.). Hold (ct. &). Small step to R on R (meas. 2,
              ct. 1). Hop on R (ct. 2). Next step starts with hop
              on R and moves slightly to L. Step is done thusly
              when facing ctr. and moving to side. When mov-
              ing fwd. or bwd., the small steps are done either
              fwd. or bwd.

PATTERN

Measures

Figure I. Side Step

1   Hop on L (ct. 1). Small step to R on R (ct. &). Step
          L next to R (ct. 2). Hold (ct. &).

2	Small step to R on R (ct. 1). Step L next to R (ct. 2).
3-4	Repeat action of meas. 2 two more times (3 in all). On last step on L, put no wt.
5-8	Repeat action of meas. 1-4 but start with hop on R and move to L. Put no wt. on last step on R.

Figure II. Forward, Back, and Circle

1-4	Beg. with hop on L, dance 2 Dunda Steps fwd. twd. ctr.
5-8	Beg. with hop on L, dance 2 Dunda Steps bwd. away from ctr.
9-12	Beg. with hop on L, dance 2 Dunda Steps in a small circle (actually more of a horseshoe in shape) moving CW and always facing ctr. of the large circle.
13-16	Repeat action of meas. 9-12, Fig. II, but move CCW in the small circle.

Figure III. Interlude

1	Step to R side on R (ct. 1). Step L across behind R (ct. 2).
2-4	Repeat action of meas. 1, Fig. III, three more times (4 in all).

Repeat dance from beginning to end of music.

BUNIEVACHKO MOMACHKO
("Momachko Kolo")

SOURCE:	This is a kolo from Subotitsa, a city in Bachka, which is a province in Serbia. Subotitsa is next to the Hungarian border and the dance shows much Hungarian influence. In the title, "Bunievachko" refers to the people of this region and "Momachko" refers to "bachelors."
MUSIC:	Record — Kolo Festival, KF-4801, Bunievachko Momachko Kolo. Folk Dancer MH 3022 (8 meas.

intro.). Any good recording of Bunievachko Momachko Kolo that follows the A, B, C sequence. The music has three musical strains — A, B, C, each of eight measures duration.

FORMATION: Sets of 3, 1 M between 2 W in a line of 3, all facing the same direction. All sets face the same direction, and may be arranged in lines or columns all facing the same direction, or all facing LOD in one circle. Keep at least 5 ft. clearance from the set in front. M has 1 arm around the waist of each W, holding her outside hand on her outside hip. Both W place their inside hand on the M's nearest shoulder. Unless otherwise indicated, hands are on hips with palms out.

STEPS: *"Basic Step"* for M and W: using small steps throughout, step swd. R on R (ct. 1), close L to R (ct. &), step swd. on R to R (ct. 2), lift L and swing heel over R instep with L toe turned outward by movement of the ankle, at same time slightly lift and lower R heel (ct. &). To move to the L, start L and use opp. ftwork. The basic step is always done with the trio moving swd., alternating R and L, even though the pattern sequence may move the sets fwd., bwd., or turning. Other steps described below.

PATTERN
Music 2/4

Measures

4 meas.   Introduction. Dancers stand in formation, taking trio pos.

Figure I. Basic Steps in Place

A   1-8   All do 8 basic steps in place, starting R.

Figure II. Forward and Back

B   1-4   All do 4 basic steps fwd., starting R.

     5-8   All do 4 basic steps bwd., starting R.

Figure III. Turning in Line

C   1-4   All do 4 basic steps turning in line CW, once around, starting R.

     5-8   All do 4 basic steps turning in line CCW, to place, starting R.

Figure IV. Women's Change — Long Sequence

In this sequence the 2 W exchange places, with the R W passing between the L W and M. After the exchange, which takes 2 meas., all do 2 meas. in place. During the exchange each W makes 1 turn around so that she faces the M throughout the exchange (R W turns CCW, L W turns C W). M assists W to start by guiding each W with his hand at her back. Both W start with inside ft. (R W must shift wt.). W hands are removed from M's shoulders during the change only. L. W does the counterpart of R W, passing outside R W. 4 changes of place occur, with the W finishing in their original pos.

A-1   R W steps to L with stamp L (ct. 1), small hop L (ct. &), step R (ct. 2), step L (ct. &). R W turns CCW as she does this ftwork and progresses across in front of M. At end of this meas. she is directly in front of M, facing him. Simultaneously L W starts with R ft., and does counterpart of R W, passing outside R W. M steps bwd. with stamp R, assisting W to change by gently guiding each with the hand which was around her waist (ct. 1), small hop R (ct. &), step L in place (ct. 2), step R in place (ct. &).

2   R W continues CCW turn with stamp R to R (ct. 1), small hop R (ct. &), step L (ct. 2), step R (ct. &). R W

has now completed 1 CCW turn and has progressed to L W orig. pos., places inside hand on M L shoulder.

Simultaneously, L W continues CW turn and using opp. ft. from R W finishes on R side of M, with L hand on his R shoulder. M stamps L in place (ct. 1); hop L (ct. &), step R in place (ct. 2), step L slightly fwd. to rejoin line of 3 (ct. &). M places arms around both W waists.

3   M and L W stamp R in place (ct. 1), hop R (ct. &), step L in place (ct. 2), step R in place (ct. &).
R W does counterpart of L W, starting L.

4   M and L W stamp L (cts. 1, &), stamp R (cts. 2, &).
R W stamps R (cts. 1, &), stamps L (cts. 2, &).

5-8   Repeat action of Fig. IV, meas. 1-4, but with former R W doing action described for L W, and former L W doing action described for R W.

B 1-8   Repeat action of Fig. IV, meas. 1-8, except with the following change of pos. on meas. 8. On meas. 8 M removes arms from around W and W remove hands from M shoulders. M does stamp L, stamp R, moving fwd. to take his place in front of W, while W join inside hands and dance steps indicated for meas. 8.

Figure V. Man's Solo

C 1   M jumps to stride pos. (ct. 1), jump and click heels together (ct. &), return to stride pos. (ct. 2), jump and click heels together (ct. &).

2   M lands on R ft. (ct. 1), stamp L toe in place (ct. &), stamp R toe in place (ct. 2), hold and shift wt. to both ft. (ct. &).

3-8   M repeats action of Fig. V, meas. 1-2 three times. On meas. 8 M moves bwd. to rejoin line of 3.

Women's Part

1   R W steps L on L (ct. 1), lift flexed R ankle in front
     of L instep, bending L knee slightly with small dip
     (ct. &), step R on R (ct. 2), lift flexed L ankle in front
     of R instep, bending R knee slightly with small dip
     (ct. &). L W does counterpart of R W, starting R.

2   R W steps L on L (ct. 1), lift flexed R ankle in front
     of R instep, bending L knee slightly with small dip
     (ct. &), holding. R ankle in same pos. repeat 1 knee
     bend (ct. 2), repeat L knee bend (ct. &). Three slight
     knee bends are done in total.
     L W does counterpart of R W, starting R.

3-4 Starting with opps. ft. (R W with R, L W with L),
     repeat action of Fig. V, meas. 1-2.

5-8 Repeat action of Fig. V, meas. 1-4. At end of meas.
     8 R W shifts wt. to L.
     Note: On this sequence, both W roll their R shoul-
     der fwd. when on R ft., and L shoulder fwd. when
     on L. This reflects the Hungarian influence on the
     dance.

     Figure VI. Forward and Back
A 1-8 Repeat action of Fig. II.

     Figure VII. Women's Change — short sequence
     The W exchange places in a manner similar to Fig.
     IV, except with the timing being halved.

B 1   R W steps to L with stamp L (ct. 1), hop L (ct. &),
        step R (ct. 2), step L (ct. &). During above ftwork, R
        W makes one complete CCW turn and progresses
        across in front of M to finish in L W pos. (For sim-
        plification, W may omit the turn and move straight
        across.)
        L W does counterpart, starting R, and passing out-
        side of R W.

2   Both W place inside hands on M shoulders, and all assume orig. pos. Orig. R W stamps R (ct. 1, &), stamp L (ct. 2, &). L W does counterpart, starting L. Simultaneously M steps bwd., with stamp R, assisting W to change by gently guiding each with the hand which was around her waist (ct. 1), small hop R (ct. &), step L in place (ct. 2), step R fwd. to rejoin line of 3 (ct. &).
Stamp L in place (cts. 1, &), stamp R in place (cts. 2, &).

3-4   All perform the actions of Fig. VII, meas. 1-2, starting opp. ft. and with W in exchanged pos.

5-8   All repeat action of Fig. VII, meas. 3-4. On meas. 8 M takes pos. in front of W, and W join inside hands.

Figure VIII. Man's Solo

C 1-8   Repeat action of Fig. V, or M may do any acceptable solo variation (3 variations are given at end of description.)
Use the following sequence to the end of the record:
Music A: Forward and Back, or Turning in Line.
Music B: W Change — Short Sequence.
Music C: M solo — any of the variations.
Note: On the last time through the Kolo Festival record omits Music B.

Man's Solo — Variation I

C 1-8   W perform action previously described. M repeat action of Fig. V, but make 180° turn on each heel-click jump. Thus, M makes 4 complete CW (or CCW) turns.

Man's Solo — Variation II
W perform action previously described.

C 1   M with wt. on L, stamp R along L (ct. 1), raise R with flexed ankle and swing in front of L ankle, at same time rising on L toe (ct. &), stamp R along L, at same time lowering L heel to floor (ct. 2), raise R with flexed ankle and click to side of L ankle, at same time rising on L toe (ct. &).

2   Stamp R along L (ct. 1), raise R with flexed ankle and swing behind L ankle, at same time rising on L toe (ct. &), stamp R along L (ct. 2), stamp L along R, keeping wt. on R (ct. &).

3-4   With wt. on R, stamp L, and repeat action of meas. 1-2, using L.

5-8   Repeat action of meas. 1-4, rejoining W on meas. 8.

Man's Solo — Variation III
W perform action previously described.

C 1-8   Repeat action of Fig. V, merely raising ankles from floor to click heels. On meas. 2 do 4 slight stamps, with no hold ct.

STARO RATARSKO
(Stah ro Rah Tar sko)
(Old Farmer's Dance)

SOURCE: Learned in Belgrade by Anatol Joukowsky. Like Zabarka, Moravac and Senjacko, Staro Ratarsko belongs to the family of Kolos known as "U Sest Koraka."

MUSIC: Record — Jugoton C-6211 Ratarsko Kolo 2/4 time. No introduction.

FORMATION: Open kolo (broken circle). Hands joined and held down. Face a little L of Line of Direction (CCW).

PATTERN

Measures

Figure I (Promenade)

1   Step R in LOD (ct. 1). Step L in LOD (ct. 2).

2   Facing ctr., step R to R side (ct. 1). Close L to R (no wt.) (ct. 2).

3   Step L to L (ct. 1). Close R to L (no wt.) (ct. 2).

4   Step R to R (ct. 1). Close L to R (no wt.) (ct. 2).

5-8   Repeat action of meas. 1-4, but start with L to L (RLOD).

9-16   Repeat action of meas. 1-8.

Figure II

1   Facing ctr., move diagonally fwd. and to the R. Step R, bending knee (cts. 1, &). Hop R (ct. 2). Step L in front of R (ct. &). Hop is usually modified into just a heel lift.

2   Hold (ct. 1). Step R to R (ct. &). Step L in front of R (cts. 2, &). Movement is still diagonally fwd. and to the R.

3   Moving back out of circle, step back on R (cts. 1, &). Step back on L (ct. 2). Step back on R (ct. &).

4   Still moving out of circle, step L (cts. 1, &). Step R (ct. &).

5-8   Repeat action of meas. 1-4, but start L, diagonally fwd. and to L.

9-16   Repeat action of meas. 1-8.

Figure III

1   Step R to R (cts. 1, &). Hop on R (ct. 2). Step L behind R (ct. &).

2   Hold (ct. 1). Step R to R (ct. &). Step L behind R (cts. 2, &).

3   Step R and extend L fwd. and low (cts. 1, &). Step L and extend R (ct. 2). Step R and extend L (ct. &). Meas. 3 is danced in place.

4   Moving to L, step L (cts. 1, &). Step R behind L (ct. 2). Step L to L, bending knee (ct. &).

5-16   Repeat action of meas. 1-4 three times (4 in all). On repeat of pattern, first step on R (ct. 1, &) is behind L. Repeat dance from beginning three times.

KOLO FROM VRANJE
(Vran-yeh)
(Women's Round Dance)

SOURCE: Vranje is in south Serbia. This was originally a women's dance.

MUSIC: Record — Muzicki Pejsazi Jugoslavije. RTB LOP 6 Side A, Band 1.
This kolo is in 9/8 meter, consisting of 2/8, 3/8, 2/8, 2/8, so that 4 beats are felt. Each meas. will be written as having 4 cts. with ct. 2 underlined to note that it is of longer duration.

FORMATION: Dancers in a broken circle with hands joined by interlocking last 2 fingers of R hand through last 2 fingers of neighbor's L. Elbows are bent with palms twd. ctr.

PATTERN

Measures

1   Step R to R side (ct. 1). Step L across behind R *(ct. 2)*. Step R to R side (ct. 3). Step L across in front of R (ct. 4).

2-3   Repeat action of meas. 1 two more times.

4   Release hands, keeping them at shoulder height.

Turn R on 4 walking steps, making a small circle.
Keep repeating the above pattern. As dance pro-
gresses, the step on the R in meas. 1-3 becomes a
step-hop.
Step R to R side (ct. 1). Small hop on R (ct. &). Step
L across behind R *(ct. 2)*. Step R to R side (ct. 3).
Small hop on R (ct. &). Step L across in front of R
(ct. 4).

DUNDA KOLO

SOURCE: Learned and danced in Serbia by Anatol Joukow-
            sky during the period from 1920-1940. The sig-
            nificance of Dunda has long been lost. This ver-
            sion is arranged by him.

MUSIC: Records — Kolo Festival KF 812-B Dunda Kolo.
            Kolo in Beograda Vol. I, Side 1, Band 2 2/4 meter.

FORMATION: Dancers in open circle, facing ctrs., leader at R
            end. Hands joined and held down.

STEPS: *Side-Close:* (to R) Step R to R side (ct. 1). Close
            L to R (ct. 2). Next step would be again R.
            Syncopated Threes: Step R in place, bending knee
            (cts. 1, &). Step L beside R (ct. 2). Step R in place
            (ct. &). Also done beg. with L. Rhythm is "slow-
            quick-quick." Same step found in Moravac, Za-
            barka, U Sest Koraka.
            Dunda Step: (1 step to 2 meas.) Described in body
            of dance but basically the same step as used in
            Vasino Kolo of Serbian Medley #3.

PATTERN

Measures

            Introduction
1-8   Dance 8 side-close steps to R.

            Figure I. Threes and Side-Close
1-4   Four Syncopated 3's in place beg. R.

5-8   Four Side-Close Steps to R.

9-16   Repeat action of meas. 1-8 (Fig. I).

            Figure II. Walking
1   Step R to R side (ct. 1). Step L across in front of R
            (ct. 2).

2   Step R to R side (ct. 1). Step L across in back of R (ct. 2).

3-4 Repeat action of meas. 2 (Fig. II) two more times. Cue: Side-Front (once) Side-Back (3 times).

5-16 Repeat action of meas. 1-4 (Fig. II) 3 times (4 in all). On all walking steps there is a slight body turn as the shoulder follows the crossing ft.

Figure III. Threes and Side-Close
1-16 Repeat action of Fig. I.

Figure IV. Walking
1-8 Repeat action of Fig. II meas. 1-8 only.

Figure V. Dunda Step Facing Ctr.
1   Hop on L (ct. 1). Small step to R on R (ct. &). Step L next to R (ct. 2). Hold ct. &.

2   Small step to R on R (ct. 1). Hop on R (ct. 2).

3-4 Repeat action of meas. 1-2 (Dunda Step) beg. hop on R, and moving L.

5-16 Repeat action of meas. 1-4 three more times (8 Dunda Steps in all).

Figure VI. Walking Var. I
1   Step R to R side (ct. 1). Step L across in front of R (ct. 2).

2   Repeat action of meas. 1 (Fig. VI).

3   Step R to R side (ct. 1). Step L across in back of R (ct. 2).

4   Repeat action of meas. 3 (Fig. VI).

5-8 Repeat action of meas. 1 (Fig. VI) 4 times. Cue: Sd.-Fr. (2 times) Sd.-Bk (2 times) Sd.-Fr. (4 times).

9-10 Repeat action of meas. 3 (Fig. VI) twice.

11-12   Repeat action of meas. 1 (Fig. VI) twice.

13-16   Repeat action of meas. 3 (Fig. VI) 4 times. End facing RLOD.
Cue: Sd.-Bk. (2 times) Sd.-Fr. (2 times) Sd.-Bk. (4 times).

Figure VII. Dunda Step Travelling in LOD

1   Hop on L, facing RLOD (ct. 1). Step back on R in LOD (ct. &). Step back on L in LOD (ct. 2).

2   Step on R (ct. 1). Hop on R (ct. 2). Turn to face LOD on Step-hop.

3   Repeat action of meas. 1 but beg. hop on R. Face and travel LOD.

4   Step-hop on L, turning to face LOD.

5-16   Repeat action of meas. 1-4 (Fig. VII) 3 times (8 Dunda Steps in all). On last Step-hop end facing ctr.

Figure VIII. Interlude

1   Step R to R side (ct. 1). Step L across in back of R (ct. 2).

2-3   Repeat action of meas. 1 two more times.

4   Small step R on R (ct. 1). Step L next to R (ct. &). Step R in place (ct. 2).

5-8   Repeat action of meas. 1-4 but beg. L and travel L.

Figure IX. Walking Var. II

1   Step R to R side (ct. 1). Step L across in front of R (ct. 2).

2   Step R to R side (ct. 1). Step L across in back of R (ct. 2).

3-6   Repeat action of meas. 1 four times.
Cue: Sd.-Fr., Sd.-Bk., Sd.-Fr. (4 times).

7   Repeat action of meas. 2.

8   Repeat action of meas. 1.

9-12   Repeat action of meas. 2 four times.
          Cue: Sd.-Bk., Sd.-Fr., Sd.-Bk. (4 times).

13-24   Repeat action of meas. 1-12 (Fig. IX). End facing
          RLOD.

          Figure X. Dunda Step Travelling in LOD
1-16   Repeat action of Fig. VII.

VRANJANKA
(Dance from Vranje)

SOURCE: This version of Vranjanka was learned in Serbia
              by Anatol Joukowsky.

MUSIC: Record — Muzicki   Pejsazi   Jugoslavije.   RTB
              LOP6, Side B, Band 4.

FORMATION: Broken circle, hands joined and held fwd. about
              shoulder height with arms gently curved. Leader
              carries handkerchief in R hand. Dance is in 3/4
              meter.

PATTERN

Measures
16 meas.   Introduction.

1   Step to R on R (ct. 1). Lift on R ft. (modified hop)
           (ct. 2). Step L across in front of R (ct. 3).

2   Step to R on R (ct. 1). Step to L on L (ct. 2). Step R
           across in front of L (ct. 3).

3   Step to L on L with flex of L knee, turning body
           slightly to R (ct. 1). Shifting R ft. so heel is twd. L
           ankle, flex knees (ct. 2). Flex knees again (ct. 3).

4   Step R in place with flex of R knee, turning body
           slightly to L (ct. 1). Shifting L ft. so heel is twd. R
           ankle, flex knees (ct. 2). Flex knee again (ct. 3).

5   Step L beside R (ct. 1). Step R in place (ct. 2). Step
         L in place (ct. 3).
         Variation for M: meas. 5 — Step L beside R (ct. 1).
         Bend R leg with R knee turned to R, bringing lower
         R leg behind L calf (cts. 2, 3). Legs form a figure 4.

KARANFILE
(Kar ahn fee leh)
(Coronation Dance)

SOURCE: Karanfile is a dance from Kosmet, a region of
               southern Serbia.

MUSIC: Record — Jogoton C6447. 12 measure introduc-
               tion.

FORMATION: Open kolo (broken circle). Hands joined and held
               down. Face in LOD (CCW).

STEPS: Every step is done with a plié or bend of knee.
               Wt. is on balls of ft. with heels close to ground.
               Karanfile is in 4/8 meter. Sometimes 1/8 and 1/8
               combined to give a longer ct. to the step.

PATTERN

Introduction 12 measures. Stand in place.

Count   *Measure I*
2/8 (S)   Step L in LOD (cts. 1, 2).

2/8 (S)   Step R in LOD (cts. 3, 4).

           Measure II
1/8 (Q)   Step L in LOD (ct. 1).

1/8 (Q)   Step R in LOD (ct. 2).

2/8 (S)   Step L in LOD (cts. 3, 4).

           Measure III
2/8 (S)   Step R twd. ctr. (face ctr.) (cts. 1, 2).

2/8 (S) Lift R heel and raise L leg with knee slightly bent (cts. 3, 4). Joined hands should naturally rise on this motion.

Measure IV

1/8 (Q) Step bwd. on L (out of circle) and lift R knee, turning it to L (ct. 1).

1/8 (Q) Turn R knee to R (ct. 2). Movement of knee should turn body. Leg does not move just from hip joint.

1/8 (Q) Turn R knee to L (ct. 3). Body turns with knee.

1/8 (Q) Step R in LOD (ct. 4). Joined hands have returned to beginning pos.
    Repeat these four meas. until end of music.

CARLAMA UZICKA
(Char lah meh u gee tse)

SOURCE: Carlama is done in Serbia and Bosnia and has many variations. Originally it was a man's dance. Today both men and women dance in the same line. Learned in Serbia by Anatol Joukowsky.

MUSIC: Record — Jugoton J-1002. 4/4 time. No introduction.

FORMATION: Open circle with hands joined and down. Stand facing center.

STEPS: Each step is done with a plié or bend of knee. In Figure I hands swing naturally forward and back.

PATTERN

Measures

Figure I

1 Step R fwd. (6 inches) (ct. 1). Step L in place (ct. 2). Step R next to L (ct. 3). Lift R heel (ct. 4).

2   Repeat action of meas. 1 starting L.

3-8 Repeat action of meas. 1 and 2, 3 times (4 times in all).

Figure II

1   Step R swd. (ct. 1). Close L to R (ct. 2). Step R swd. (ct. &). Close L to R (ct. 3). Step R swd. (ct. &). Close L to R (ct. 4).

2-3 Repeat action of meas. 1 twice.

4   Step swd. R (ct. 1). Close L to R (ct. 2). Step swd. R (ct. &). Close L to R (ct. 3). Step swd. R and bend knee (ct. 4).

5-8 Repeat action of meas. 1-4, starting L.

Figure III

1-8 Repeat action of Figure I, meas. 1-8.

Figure IV

1-4 Repeat action of Figure II, meas. 1, 4 times.

Figure V

1   Facing LOD leap onto R (cts. 1, 2). Step L slightly ahead of R (ct. 3). Step R close to L (ct. 4). On leap, bend knee and lift it high.

2   Repeat action of meas. 1, starting L.

3-16 Repeat action of meas. 1 and 2, 7 times (8 in all). Note: During this figure leader serpentines the line about the floor. By the 16th meas. he must be close enough to the end of the line to join hands and form a complete circle. The remainder of the dance is done in a closed circle. Repeat alternately Figure I and Figure II to end of record.

KATANKA
(Serbian Square Dance)

SOURCE: Learned in Pirot, Serbia near the Bulgarian border by Anatol Joukowsky.

MUSIC: Record — Kolo Festival RRH80P-1503 (Vol. 3). Second dance. 3/4 time.

FORMATION: Two couples dancing anywhere in hall. Ptrs. stand opposite, facing each other, about 6 to 8 ft. apart. M(1) (see diagram). At start, handkerchief is W(2) M(2) held by both hands behind back (hip level). W(1).

STEPS: *Basic step:* Step R (ct. 1). Step L (ct. 2). Step R (accent), bending R knee (ct. 3). Next step would start with L. Danced in place, turning or moving. As dance progresses, experienced dancers may add flourishes to basic step. Start each figure on R ft. There are many figures that may be used for Katanka, but only 4 common ones are given here. It is not necessary to use figures in order given. Sequences may be repeated. M(1), the leader, should signal start of new sequence by wave of handkerchief in R hand. M(1) starts action of each sequence.

Note: Although dance is now played in 3/4 time, in all probability it was originally done in 7/16 time which explains the accent on ct. 3 as it is done today.

PATTERN

Measures

Figure I

1-8 Dance 8 basic steps in place starting R. Handkerchief behind back during Figure I and II.

9-12   All go to ctr. on 4 basic steps.

13-16   All back up to place on 4 basic steps.

Figure II. Changing Places

1-4   Cpl. 1 change places on 4 basic steps. During figure always start R and pass R shoulders. Cpl. 2 dance in place.

5-8   Cpl. 2 change places on 4 basic steps. Cpl. 1 turn 1/2 R (CW) to face ctr. on 4 basic steps.

9-12   Cpl. 1 return to place on 4 basic steps. Cpl. 2 turn 1/2 R (CW) to face ctr. on 4 basic steps.

13-16   Cpl. 2 return to place on 4 basic steps. Turn R to face ctr. on last basic step. Cpl. 1 turn 1/2 turn R (CW) to face ctr. on 4 basic steps.

Figure III. Single Turn

1-8   Hold handkerchief by both hands in front at eye level. All turn R (CW) in place on 8 basic steps. Number of turns up to dancer but slow down on meas. 7-8 so that following change of direction is not too abrupt.

9-16   Turn L (CCW) in place on 8 basic steps.

Figure IV. Turn With Partner

1-8   Handkerchief again behind back. Cpl. 1 dance to ctr. on 2 basic steps and join R hands. Make one turn to R (CW) under joined R hands on 4 basic steps. Back up to place on 2 basic steps. Cpl. 2 dances in place. On turn, handkerchief is held in inactive hand.

9-16   Repeat action of meas. 1-8 with Cpl. 2 making the turn.

17-24   Repeat action of meas. 1-8. Cpl. 1 make turn but join L hands. Turn L (CCW) under joined L hands.

25-32   Repeat action of meas. 1-8. Cpl. 2 make turn but join
            L hands.
            To fit the listed recording it is suggested that Fig.
            I-IV be danced as given twice through. The third
            time dance Fig. I, II, III, and end with following
            pattern.

            Figure V. All Circle
1-8   Using basic step, all move in and to L. As soon as
            possible, join hands and continue circling to L.
            Handkerchief hangs from R hand (even though it is
            joined with neighbor).

                            METELIKUM
                          (Meh tay lee koom)
                      (Albania Minorities' Dance)

SOURCE: Metelikum is Albanian girl's dance. This dance
              is of Turkish origin.

MUSIC: Record — Jugoton C6448 Metelikum. 9/8 time.
              No introduction.

FORMATION: Open kolo (broken circle). Each holds handker-
              chief in R hand, other end held by neighbor.
              Hands held up, elbows bent, with handkerchiefs
              at about eye level. There is enough tension so
              handkerchiefs do not sag. Leader's handkerchief
              hangs from R hand. Face a little L of Line of
              Direction (LOD).

STEPS: Dance is in 9/8 rhythm which may be counted 1
              2, 1 2, 1 2, 1 2 3 (2/8, 2/8, 2/8, 3/8). Dance uses
              3 basic steps.
              Step I: Face a little L of LOD and progress in
              LOD, Step R in LOD (2/8). Step L in LOD
              (2/8). Step R in LOD (2/8). Step diagonally back
              on L and touch R ankle to L ankle (3/8). On last
              step on L, direction is to Reverse LOD (RLOD)

and a little out of ctr. Face to ctr. Knees are bent
and R ft. just clears floor. Step I repeats exactly.

Step II: Step R to R side (2/8). Cross L in front
of R (2/8). Step back R in place (2/8). Step L
next to R (1/8). Step R in place (2/8). Next step
starts with L to L side.

Step III: Step R to R side (2/8). Close L to R
(2/8). Step R to R side (2/8). Step L next to R
and touch R ankle to L ankle, knees bent (3/8).
Step repeats exactly.

PATTERN

Measures

Figure I

1-14 Moving in LOD, dance Step I fourteen times. Always start R. Takes 1 instrumental and 1 vocal sequence.

Interlude Easily recognized. Vocalist breaks from usual melody. Step to R with R. Cross L over to R side of R and make 1/2 turn R (CW). Raise arms on turn and then lower them. During next 3 fig. L arm is crossed over R. Handkerchiefs still held.
Note: This type of turn occurs 3 times during dance. There is no exact timing. Turn is unhurried and should take most of the interlude music.

Figure II

1-8 Dance Step II eight times, alternately R and L (4 to each side). Done to vocal.

Figure III

1-9 Moving to R, dance Step III nine times. Always start R. No vocal.

Figure IV

1-5 Dance Step II five times, alternately R and L. Done to vocal.

Interlude   Step to L with L. Cross R over to L side of L and make 1/2 turn L (CCW). Arms are raised for turn and then lowered into beginning pos.

Figure V

1-3   Dance Step I three times. Always start R.

4   Turn R (CW) once thusly: Step R (2/8). Step L (2/8). Step R (2/8). Step L and bring R to L, ankles touching (3/8). Actual turn should take only the first 3 steps. Drop handkerchief held in L hand during turn and take again at end of turn.

5-20   Repeat action of meas. 1-4 four more times.

21-22   Dance Step I two times.

Interlude   Use same turn as in first interlude.

Figure VI

1-7   Dance Step II seven times, alternately R and L. Done to vocal.

CHAPTER FOUR

BULGARIA

The native dance of Bulgaria is one of the most significant and important expressions of the culture of that country, and it reflects the life of the Bulgarian people.

Virtually the only outlet for popular creative expression in the past period of Turkish domination, is the dance, the dress and the song. In essence Bulgarian native dance as well as the other characteristic documents of Bulgarian culture show its Slav origin. There are traces, however, of the influence of the Mediterranean and other people in close contact with Bulgaria.

With the great changes after the liberation from Turkish domination in the second part of XIX Century many of the old traditional dances and costumes vanished, and some underwent much alteration.

The national dance is a product of geographic, economic, religious and ethnographic factors. With the music and costumes it is a concrete expression of the people's creative power.

The customs of the people are tied in irrevocably with the dance of the people. The people are characterized by happy families with many children and cattle. Because many customs are so important to the evolution of the Bulgarian dance, some are described here. The customs that passed on from generation to generation were fully observed until the end of the first World War, after which they began to deteriorate and to be followed only partially or in a modified form.

This is particularly true of the Christmas customs, one of which is celebrated with a large dinner on Christmas Eve. All the food available in the house and from the fields is laid on

the table. This includes peppers, pastry, cabbage leaves stuffed
with mince meat and rice, homemade breads and cheeses, together with millet, oats, and many other homemade foods. The
floor is covered with straw and the Christmas Eve dinner is
served here. Tokens placed in the pies and pastries provide
fortunes for all those present just before the dinner. A big tree
stump called "budnik," yule log, is placed on the hearth and
the fire is maintained throughout the entire evening.

Christmas carolers, festively dressed, travel from home to
home singing Christmas carols very much the same as we do in
the United States. The lyrics are dedicated to the housewives,
young men or women, bachelors, widows, widowers, school

boys, shepherds. The Christmas singers are offered presents and coins which are usually collected for public needs and village improvements. The text of the songs realistically reflects the local way of life with its economic forms and social relations. As a rule, these songs are gay and often abound in humor.

New Year's, too, has its evening feast and is almost a repetition of the Christmas customs where the fortune of the family is foretold. Specially dressed for the occasion, and armed with their "sourvaknitsi," which is cornel-twigs, the children make the rounds of neighbors and relatives, striking them on the back and expressing good wishes for the New Year. The cornel-twig used for this custom is full of sprouts and is adorned with colorful ribbons, coins, cracked maize and geranium.

The early spring customs start on February 14th. On this day the vine growers, armed with pruning knives, food, wine-and-brandy flasks go into their vineyards and solemnly prune several vines, clipping off last year's sticks. General feasting and merry-making follows. In many villages the custom prevails to go out to the vineyards on horses, mules and donkeys, staging handicap races. This is one of the merriest holidays and wine flows in abundance.

The next big holiday is Shrovetide, which is celebrated in different regions, and is most commonly known as "Koukeri." Usually they represent groups of costumed and masked young or adult men. The gatherings depict social groups typical of the past, such as military brigades and rebel bands.

The "Koukeri" is made up in a great variety of costumes, depending upon what they represent; the chieftains are dressed in military uniforms or in old richly ornamented costumes; others appear as policemen, and Gypsies, and others wear many different masks which often are artistic in design and execution. Sometimes, to achieve a particular effect, the masks are adorned with bird feathers, sheep or goat horns, bean pods and seeds.

The "Koukeri" groups are always well-organized, have strictly established rules and owe complete obedience to their chief. This custom is more than mere entertainment, for it is supposed to be conducive to good crops, fertility of the soil and health in the household.

In the evening big fires are lighted in the streets or outside the village. A similar idea underlies the March 1st custom of burning the garbage in courtyards and gardens early in the morning. People walk around the fire beating some iron objects and intoning, "Get away serpents and lizards, for Grandma March is coming with the broom and will smash your heads."

One of the most solemn rites is that performed by young girls on St. Lazarus Day before Easter. Gay and noisy, poetic and colorful, it is celebrated practically all over Bulgaria, with minor variations from region to region. Groups of girls travel from house to house singing folk songs on this occasion. The girls wear all kinds of ornaments; rings, bracelets, necklaces and artificial feathers. In every home they sing as many songs as there are family members. Each song corresponds to the age, profession, social status of the person in whose honor it is sung. After performing their repertory, the girls receive an egg each, some money and other souvenirs, bid the family goodbye and visit the next household. A house honored by the visit of the St. Lazarus girls is considered happy; there will be family happiness throughout the year, full beehives, good crops, prolific cattle and joy.

There are many other customs of expelling the evil spirits and for giving thanks for full and rich crops, as well as happiness in the family and in the villages.

A custom which is quite local in character is that of the "Nestinarki." These are the fire dances practiced in the past in a few villages only, and today solely in the village of Bulgari in Southeast Bulgaria. People dance to the tunes of a drum and bagpipe, and gradually some of them fall into a trance and dance the so-called Nestinarska Rachenitsa, moaning and wailing. The same evening live coals are spread on the village square and a village Horo is danced around the fire to the tunes of the same bagpipe and drum. The leader of the Horo carries the icon of Constantine and Helen.

The autumn customs are usually thanksgiving feasts at which the food and drink produced in summer is placed on the table. An interesting autumn custom is the first sowing of the grain on St. Simeon Day, September 14th. The peasants go out then to sow the first seeds in the soil. The ploughers and cattle are ornamented with flowers, while red strings are tied on the horns of the oxen and on the plough. The plougher takes for lunch a specially baked wheat pie which he rolls on the field before eating. When breaking the pie, he first gives a piece to the cattle. All this is done with the wish that "out of this seed a thousand may be born."

Many were the customs of the Bulgarians of old, widely observed until the Balkan Wars and World War I. The Bulgarian folk customs subsequently began to disintegrate, some of them assuming a different character, while others fell into complete oblivion. Most customs that were preserved gradually lost their original religious significance and became mere entertainments. The Bulgarian dances presented herewith reflect many of these traditional customs, and are in some cases the only vestige of these customs left.

ZA POJAS
(Zah Poy as)
(By The Belt)

SOURCE: Za Pojas (by the belt) comes from the region of Nova Zagora, Bulgaria.

MUSIC: Record — XOPO 308A Novo Zagorsko Horo. 2/4 time. No introduction.

FORMATION: Open kolo (broken circle). Dancers hold neighbors by belts, L arm over R. End dancers hold handkerchief in free hand.

STEPS: Although wt. is on balls of ft., heels are close to ground. On leaps the emphasis is more on height than on distance.

PATTERN

Measures

1   Moving in LOD, leap onto R (ct. 1). Step L in front R (ct. 2).

2-3   Repeat action of meas. 1 twice (3 in all).

4   Step R to R side (ct. 1). Hop on R, swinging L across in front of R (ct. 2).

5   Step L to L side (ct. 1). Hop on L, swinging R across in front of L (ct. 2).

6   Repeat action of meas. 4 (step-hop on R).

7-9   Repeat action of meas. 1-3 but move to RLOD. Leap onto L and cross R behind.

10   Step-hop on L, swinging R.

11   Step-hop on R, swinging L.

12   Moving into ctr., step L (ct. 1), R (ct. &), L (ct. 2). Hold (ct. &).

13   Still moving into ctr., step-hop on R. On hop bend L knee and raise it high.

14-16   Move out of ctr. on 3 step-hops (L, R, L). On each hop the knee of the free leg is bent and raised high. Repeat above pattern to end of music.

GANKINO HORO
(Gana's Horo)

SOURCE: Learned in Bulgaria from the natives by Anatol Joukowsky.

MUSIC: Record — XOPO (Horo) X302-A Gankino.

FORMATION: Open circle or line. Hands joined and down.

STEPS: Every step is done with a plié or bend of knee. Weight is on balls of feet with heels close to ground.

Gankino is danced all over Bulgaria. It is one of the principal dances done in 11/16 meter. In the diagrams below, each step is shown in relation to the musical beat to which it is danced. 11/16 meter consists of 4/16, 3/16, 4/16, all in one measure. Three beats can be felt in each measure but the count is not the same as our 3/4 time because the second beat is of shorter duration than the others.

The dance is done in a 3 measure phrase while the music uses a 4 measure phrase. This basic step has endless variations.

PATTERN

Introduction: 4 meas. Stand in place.

11/16

Measures				
1	Step R	Cross L behind R	Step R	Cross L in front of R
2	Step R	Cross L behind R	Step R	Stamp L beside R, no wt. (L ft. in 3rd pos.)
3	Step L	Cross R behind L	Step L	Stamp R beside L, no wt. (R ft. in 3rd pos.)

Repeat meas. 1, 2, 3 to end of record.

YAMBOLSKA LESA

SOURCE: Yambolska Lesa (Yahm bole skah Less ah) literally means Lesa from Yambol. Yambolska Lesa was observed and danced by Anatol Joukowsky while in Bulgaria.

MUSIC: Record — XOPO 310 Yambolska Lesa. 2/4 time.

FORMATION: Lines of 6 or 8 dancers standing side by side, facing ctr. of hall. Leader at R end. Dancers hold neighbors by belts, L arm over R. End dancers hold handkerchief in free hand.
           Note: Two of the main characteristics of a Lesa (line) is a line formation and a belt hold as described above.

STEPS: *Troyna Stupka* (troy nah Stoop kah) (triple steps): Step R, step L next to R (ct. 1). (Since this is 2/4 time placed in triplets, the step on the L occurs on the third triplet of ct. 1). Step on R (ct. 2). Lift knees high (particularly M). Repeat of step starts on L. First step of ct. 1 may be in any direction.

Udari (Oo dah ree) (beating step): Strike or beat inside of R ft. against inside of L. Sole of R ft. is parallel to and just clears floor. R knee is straight. Takes 1 ct. Done only with R ft. doing the beating.

Sechi (Seh chee) (literally means "cut"). Takes 2 meas. Hopping on L, extend R, knee straight diag. across in front of L (meas. 1, cts. 1, 2). Hopping on L, extend R, knee straight, diag. across behind L (meas. 2, cts. 1, 2). Always done with hop on L.

Note: In the Pattern names, "dva" (dvah) means two and "tri" (tree) means three. The Pattern names should be learned as they describe the action to follow. The patterns vary in the number of meas. used, so the musical phrase and the pattern do not always start at the same time.

PATTERN

Measures

8   Introduction. Stand in place.

Figure I. Udari

1   Starting with small step back diag. R on R, dance 1 Troyna Stupka (triple step).

2   Starting with small step to L side with L, dance 1 Troyna Stupka step.

3   Starting with small step to R side with R, dance 1 Troyna Stupka.

4   Step fwd. on L.

5   Beat R against L (Udari) (ct. 1). Hold ct. 2.

Figure II. Dva Udari

1-4   Repeat action of Fig. I meas. 1-4.

5   Beat R against L (ct. 1). Raise R leg, knee straight, diag. fwd. R (ct. 2).

6   Beat R against L (ct. 1). Hold ct. 2.

Figure III. Tri Udari

1-4   Repeat action of Fig. I meas. 1-4.

5   Beat R against L (ct. 1). Raise R leg, knee straight, diag. fwd. R (ct. 2).

6   Repeat action of meas. 5 (Fig. III).

7   Beat R against L (ct. 1). Hold ct. 2.

Figure IV. Udari Sechi

1-4   Repeat action of Fig. I meas. 1-4.

5   Beat R against L (ct. 1). Hold ct. 2.

6-7   Hopping on L, dance 1 Sechi step (R extended diag. in front and in back of L).

Figure V. Dva Udari Sechi

1-4   Repeat action of Fig. 1 meas. 1-4.

5   Beat R against L (ct. 1). Raise R leg, knee straight, diag. fwd. R (ct. 2).

6   Beat R against L (ct. 1). Hold ct. 2.

7-10   Hopping on L, dance 2 Sechi steps.

Figure VI. Tri Udari Sechi

1-4   Repeat action of Fig. I meas. 1-4.

5   Beat R against L (ct. 1). Hold ct. 2.

6   Raise R leg, knee straight, diag. fwd. R.

7-8   Repeat action of meas. 5-6 (Fig. VI).

9   Beat R against L (ct. 1). Hold ct. 2.

10-13	Hopping on L, dance 3 Sechi steps.

Figure VII. Skochi Udari Sechi
Skochi (skeh chee) as used in this dance means to jump.

1-3	Repeat action of Fig. I meas. 1-3. Do not include meas. 4.
4	Jump fwd. from R to land on R (Skochi) (ct. 1). Close L to R (ct. 2).
5	Beat R against L (ct. 1). Hold ct. 2.
6-7	Hopping on L dance 1 Sechi step.

Figure VIII. Dva Skochi Udari Sechi

1-3	Repeat action of Fig. I meas. 1-3.
4	Jump fwd. from R to land on R (ct. 1). Close L to R (no wt.) (ct. 2).
5	Repeat action of meas. 4 (Fig. VIII) but put wt. on. L
6	Beat R against L (ct. 1). Hold ct. 2.
7	Raise R leg, knee straight, diag. fwd. R.
8	Beat R against L (ct. 1). Hold ct. 2.
9-12	Hopping on L, dance 2 Sechi steps.

Figure IX. Tri Skochi Udari Sechi

1-3	Repeat action of Fig. I meas. 1-3.
4	Jump fwd. from R to land on R (ct. 1). Close L to R (no wt.) (ct. 2).
5	Repeat action of meas. 4 (Fig. IX).
6	Repeat action of meas. 4 (Fig. IX) but put wt. on L.
7	Beat R against L (ct. 1). Hold ct. 2.
8	Raise R leg, knee straight, diag. fwd. R.

9   Beat R against L (ct. 1). Raise R leg, knee straight, diag. fwd. R (ct. 2).

10   Beat R against L (ct. 1). Hold ct. 2.

11-16   Hopping on L, dance 3 Sechi steps.

17   Stamp flat of R ft. next to L (ct. 1). Hold ct. 2.

18   With small hop on L, raise R leg, knee straight, diag. fwd. R.

19   Stamp flat of R next to L (ct. 1) Hold ct. 2.

20   With small hop on L, raise R leg, knee straight, diag. fwd. R.

21   Stamp R next to L (no wt.) (ct. 1). Repeat stamp (no wt.) (ct. 2).

22   Stamp R next to L (ct. 1). Hold ct. 2.

Figure X. Verni Osem
Verni Osem (behr nee Oh sem) literally translated means "back eight."

1   Hop on R and step back on L (ct. 1). Hop on L and step back on R (ct. 2).

2-4   Repeat action of meas. 1 (Fig. X) 3 more times.

5   No action.

Start dance from beginning.

RACHENITSA

Rachenitsa is the liveliest of the Bulgarian dances and is known and danced throughout Bulgaria. There is no set pattern, the dancer giving rein to his fancy, improvising on the basic steps, being limited only by his endurance. The dance may be done by one man or he may be joined by others. It is essentially a solo dance as the patterns used depend upon the whim of each dancer and dancers do not necessarily do the same step at the same time. There is a feeling of rivalry between dancers. The fact that someone is dancing on the floor with him spurs the dancer on to greater heights. Usually an admiring circle is formed about the dancer or dancers to encourage them with shouts or occasional handclapping. As excitement mounts, a call of "ee-hoo-hoo" is shouted as encouragement. Dancers usually carry a "rachenik" (handkerchief) which is twirled and waved during the dance.

SOURCE: Learned by Anatol Joukowsky in Bulgaria.

MUSIC: Records — XOPO (LP) X-LP-1A Side 1 — Bands 4 and 6. Side 2 — Band 4.

FORMATION: Danced freely about area.

RHYTHM: Music is in 7/16 meter, counted 1-2, 1-2, 1-2-3. This may also be stated as 2/16, 2/16, 3/16. For simplicity's sake the ct. will be given: ct. 1 (2/16), ct. 2 (2/16), ct. 3 (3/16). In some of the steps ct. 3 is broken into two uneven parts — 2/16, 1/16.

STEPS: This is a collection of steps and not a set pattern. They are to be used in any order desired. Steps are written starting with one ft. but they can be started by either ft. that is free. At start of dance, dancers stand and get the feel of the rhythm before beginning to dance.

Counts	*Figure I. Cross Leap Step*
1 (2/16)	Lifting R knee, leap R across in front of L.
2 (2/16)	Lifting knee high, step L next to R.
3 (2/16)	Lifting knee high, step R in place.
(1/16)	Start lifting L knee in preparation for next step.
Meas. 2	Repeat action of meas. 1 but start by leaping L in front of R. This step can be done in place or in any direction. As a variation when travelling bkwd., the ft. would be crossed behind supporting leg.

Figure II. Heel Swinging
Step starts with ball of R ft. on floor in front of L. This pos. is obtained by assuming it on the last ct. of whatever step precedes it. Both knees are bent. Wt. is on L. R heel is off floor. L heel is on floor.

1 (2/16)   Swing heels to L.

2 (2/16)   Swing heels to R.

3 (3/16)   Swing heels to L.

Meas. 2   Repeat action of meas. 1 but start by swinging heels to R. Step can also be done by putting L ft. in front of R. Heels swing R on ct. 1.

Figure III. Cross Stride Step
1 (2/16)   With jump, cross R over L. Ft. slide on floor throughout step.

2 (2/16)   Jump to stride pos.

3 (3/16)   With jump, cross L over R.

1 (2/16)   Jump to stride pos.

2 (2/16)   With jump, cross R over L.

3 (3/16)   Jump to stride pos.

1 (2/16)   With jump, cross L over R.

2 (2/16)   Jump to stride pos.

3 (3/16)   With jump, cross R over L.

1 (2/16)   Jump to stride pos.

2 (2/16)   With jump, cross L over R.

3 (3/16)   Jump to stride pos.
             Takes 4 meas. to do 3 complete patterns.

Figure IV. Bulgarian Mazurka
1 (2/16)   Stepping fwd., cross R over L.

2 (2/16)   Hop on R, raising L ft. up in bk. (knee bent).

3 (2/16)   Hop on R and start crossing L.

(1/16)

Meas. 2   Repeat action of meas. 1 but start by crossing L over R. Step can be done in place or moving fwd. When moving bkwd., whole pattern is reversed with the ft. crossing behind the supporting ft.

Figure V. Little Kicks

1 (2/16)   Step L and kick R fwd.

2 (2/16)   Step R and kick L fwd.

3 (2/16)   Step L and kick R fwd.

(1/16)   Step R next to L.

Meas. 2   Repeat action of meas 1.

This step is a good travelling step.

Figure VI. Running Step

1 (2/16)   Step L.

2 (2/16)   Step R and raise L ft. up in bk. (knee bent).

3 (2/16)   Step L and extend R fwd.

(1/16)   Leap onto R.

Meas. 2   Repeat action of meas 1.

Step can be done in place or while travelling.

DAICHOVO

SOURCE: Learned and danced in Bulgaria by Anatol Joukowsky.

MUSIC: Record — Folk Dancer LP 104 MH, Side A, Band 1. Daichovo rhythm is 9/16 (2/8, 2/8, 2/8, 3/8) with 4 beats being heard and the last beat being longer. Each ct. *4* is underlined to show the longer beat.

FORMATION: Lines of dancers, 6 to 8 in each line. Leader at R end. Use belt hold with L arm over neighbor's R.

STEPS: *Basic Step:* Hop on L, bringing R knee high (ct. 1). Step R next to L (ct. 2). Step L in place (ct. 3). Step R in place (ct. *4*). Next step would start with hop on R.

Styling on slap of ft.: Full ft. should hit floor in front of supporting leg, with the knee straight. Supporting leg is bent and upper body is bent fwd.

PATTERN

Measures

4 meas.   Introduction

Figure I

1   Moving L, step R over L (ct. 1). Step L to L side (ct. 2). Repeat for cts. 3, *4*.

2   Repeat action of meas. 1.

3   In place hop on L (ct. 1), bringing R knee high. Step R next to L (ct. 2). Hop on R, bringing L knee high (ct. 3).
Step L next to R (ct. *4*).

4   Repeat action of meas. 3.

5-8   Repeat action of meas. 1-4.

Figure II

1   Moving R, step R to R side (ct. 1). Step L behind R (ct. 2). Step R to R side (ct. 3). Step L in front of R (ct. *4*).

2   Repeat action of meas. 1 (Fig. II) but on ct. *4* step L next to R.

3   Wt. on L, bend L knee and turn R heel out (ct. 1).

Knees are close together. Click R heel to L (ct. 2). Wt. on R, bend knees and turn L heel out (ct. 3). Click L heel to R (ct. *4*).

4   Repeat heel clicks of meas. 3 (Fig. II).

5-8   Repeat action of meas. 1-4 (Fig. II). End wt. on L.

Figure III

1   Step R fwd. twd. ctr. (ct. 1). Close L to R (ct. 2). Step R fwd. twd. ctr. (ct. 3). Close L to R, bending knee and lifting R in preparation for repeat of step (ct. *4*).

2-3   Repeat action of meas. 1 (Fig. III) twice.

4   Stamp R 4 times (no wt.). Knees are bent and body bent fwd.

5   Backing up, step R behind L (ct. 1). Hop on R (ct. 2). Step L behind R (ct. 3). Hop on L (ct. *4*).

6-7   Repeat action of meas. 5 (Fig. III) twice.

8   Step R behind L (ct. 1). Hop on R (ct. 2). Step L behind R (ct. 3). Slap R ft. fwd., knee straight (ct. *4*).

Figure IV

1   Turning hips a little L of ctr., wt. on L, touch R toe near L instep, R heel out (cts. 1, 2). Touch R heel in same spot, toe turned out (cts. 3, *4*). On each action there is a slight lift of L heel.

2   Dance 1 Basic Step in place, beg. hop on L and ending with hips a little R of ctr.

3-4   Repeat action of meas. 1-2 (Fig. IV) but beg. with wt. on R.

5-8   Move twd. ctr. with 4 Basic Steps beg. with hop on L.

9-16   Repeat action of meas. 1-8 (Fig. IV) but move back to place on the 4 Basic Steps.

Figure V

1   Step to R side with R heel (ct. 1). Step L behind R (ct. 2). Repeat for cts. 3, 4.

2-4   Repeat action of meas. 1 (Fig. V) but on ct. 4, meas. 4 stamp L beside R, no wt.

5-8   Repeat action of meas. 1-4 (Fig. V) but start L and move L.

9-16 Repeat action of meas. 1-8 (Fig. V).

Figure VI

1-8   Repeat action of Fig. IV, meas. 1-4 (toe-heel) twice.

Figure VII (This is an Interlude in music).

1   Slap R ft. on floor (ct. 1). Hold cts. 2, 3, 4.

2   Holding pos., shake head to R side (ct. 1), to L side (ct. 2). Repeat for cts. 3, 4.

Figure VIII

1-4   With 4 Basic Steps beg. with hop on L, making a horseshoe-shaped circle. Move CW but keep facing ctr.

5-8   With 4 Basic Steps make 1 horseshoe-shaped circle moving CCW.

9-16 Repeat action of meas. 1-8 (Fig. VIII).

Figure IX (This is same music as Introduction).

1   Slap R ft. fwd. on floor (ct. 1). Hold cts. 2-4.

2   No action.

3   Touch R toe in front of L (ct. 1). Touch R toe to R side (ct. 2). Lift leg in preparation for slap (ct. 3). Slap R ft. on floor (ct. D).

4   Repeat action of meas. 3 (Fig. IX).

Figure X

1-86 Repeat entire dance from beginning (Fig. I-IX).

Figure XI

1-7   Repeat action of Fig. I, meas. 1-7.

8   In place hop on L, bringing R knee high (ct. 1). Step
        R next to L (ct. 2). Hop on R, bringing L knee high
        (ct. 3). Slap L on floor (ct. *4*).

CHAPTER FIVE

RUMANIA

The mention of the beautiful state of Rumania brings a feeling of nostalgia to anyone who has ever visited there. The author went there many times, mostly during the summertime, just to see the villages on the Carpathian slopes of Transylvania. The endless rivers and mountains transmit a peace to the traveller.

Rumanians are very gifted in music, and this talent reflects in their dance. The dances are, for the most part, very difficult to execute. They are speedy, gay, lively. Today, several excellent Rumanian dance ensembles perform Rumanian ethnic dances. One called Rapsodia Rumina with a lovely soprano Miss Moldavan is one to see if the opportunity ever presents itself.

In travelling from one village to another trying to dig out the truth about these dances, one can see funeral dances, wedding dances, all kinds of horas. The "Ardelianas" and "Hate-ganas" and "Invertitas" and "Sirbas" although all authentic have endless variations and individuality. Each village gives its own interpretation and variation on the well-known basic form.

When a person travels north from the city of Transylvania one usually rents or buys a horse. Then at the end of the tour one sells the horse. This used to be the only kind of transportation available. Sometimes one waits a long time to see the dances and sometimes an invitation is forthcoming to stay. Once while travelling downtrail, the author was stopped by a voice, a brilliant silver soprano voice echoing from the mountains. Carefully going down hill we saw a young girl about 16 or 17 years old. She was taking water from the creek and she was singing.

She was singing like a skylark and the stream was playing the orchestra part. Stream and voice together made a beautiful panorama of the Carpathian slopes. This little girl with her embroidered blouse and short skirt, barefoot, standing in the ice cold stream made an unforgettable picture and brings to mind a dance known everywhere from Banat to Moldavia (west to east). The Hora – Jokul or Chiochirlia or lark in English. The dance imitates the free spirit of the skylark starting always slowly then going faster and faster until it reaches the furioso or climax of the dance. The basic step is not difficult, but as the speed increases and the variations are added it does call for great agility. Rumania is always associated with music and dance. It is not a nation but a profession! One of gay dancers, gay singers and happy musicians. The dance rhythm 7/8, 7/16, 13/16 is not rare in Rumanian dances.

Of all the horas we have chosen a favorite. Sarba. Sarba or Sirba is the dance reflecting the neighborhood of the State of Serbia. This is another speedy dance with a thousand variations. Another interesting Rumanian dance is the Calush. It descends from a ritual performed by a young man in the time of holy days when he raised money for school, church or some village social purpose.

Because Rumania is still essentially composed of rural population its nature is primarily peasant. The native dance of Rumania reflects this peasant quality.

JOKUL
(The Lark)

SOURCE: This is a Moldavian dance. At one time all of Moldavia was in Rumania. It is not surprising to find both countries with a dance called "The Lark." Jokul (Zhoke′ ule) was learned in Rumania (although this is the Moldavian version) by Anatol Joukowsky and was arranged by him to fit the recordings.

MUSIC: Records — Great Russian Folk Dances — Epic LC-3459 Side A, Band 4 "Jok."
Moiseyev Dance Ensemble — Bruno BR 50046 Side B, Band 1 "Zhok."
Music is in 2/4 meter.

FORMATION: Open or broken circle, leader at R end. Dancers face a little L of LOD with hands joined and held down.

STEPS: *Grapevine:* (1 step to 2 meas.). Facing ctr., step to R side on R (ct. 1). Step L across in front of R (ct. 2). Step to R side on R (meas. 2, ct. 1). Step L across behind R (ct. 2). Next step would repeat exactly. Each step done with plié or bend of knee.
Hopping Grapevine: (1 step to 2 meas.). Action is same as Grapevine Step except that each step is now a step-hop. Step to R side on R (ct. 1). Hop on R (ct. &). Step L across in front of R (ct. 2). Hop on L (ct. &). Step to R side on R (meas. 2, ct. 1). Hop on R (ct. &). Step L across behind R (ct. 2). Hop on L (ct. &).
Running Grapevine: (1 step to a meas.). Action is same as Grapevine step except that step is done double time. Because of the speed, steps are not large but knees are lifted high which gives the

look of a run. Step to R side on R (ct. 1). Step L
across in front of R (ct. &). Step to R side on R
(ct. 2). Step L across behind R (ct. &).

PATTERN

Measures

2 meas.   Introduction.

Figure I. Walk

1-2   Beg. R walk 3 steps in LOD (1 to a ct.). Step L behind R so that momentarily dancers face ctr. (meas.
2, ct. 2).

3-8   Repeat action of meas. 1-2 three more times (4 in
all).

Figure II. Grapevine

1-8   Facing ctr., dance 4 Grapevine Steps beg. R.

Figure III. Hopping Grapevine

1-8   Beg. R, dance 4 Hopping Grapevine Steps.

Figure IV. Grapevine

1-8   Beg. R, dance 4 Grapevine Steps.

Figure V. Hopping Grapevine

1-8   Beg. R, dance 4 Hopping Grapevine Steps.

Figure VI. Grapevine

1-8   Beg. R, dance 4 Grapevine Steps.

Figure VII. Running Grapevine

1-8   Beg. R, dance 8 Running Grapevine Steps.

Figure VIII. Hopping Grapevine

1-8   Beg. R, dance 4 Hopping Grapevine Steps.

Figure IX. Running Grapevine

1-8   Beg. R, dance 8 running Grapevine Steps.
Until end of music, dance now alternates between 4
Hopping Grapevine Steps and 8 Running Grapevine
Steps.

MEDGIDIA SARBA
(med gee' dee ah)

SOURCE: Medgidia (med gee' dee ah) Sarba was learned from the natives in Rumania by Anatol Joukowsky.

MUSIC: Record — Through Rumania in Song and Dance BR 50155 Side A, Band 6 Sirba 2/4 meter. No introduction.

FORMATION: Line of dancers with hands joined and held down. Leader at R end.

PATTERN

Measures

Figure I

1 Step R in place while extending L ft. fwd., almost brushing floor (ct. 1). Take heel lift on R, while bending L knee to raise L ft. in front of R leg (just below R knee) (ct. 2).

2 Step L in original place (ct. 1). Step R in place (ct. 2).

3-4 Repeat action of meas. 1-2 but start stepping on L.

5-12 Repeat action of meas. 1-4 two times. This makes 6 steps in all.

13 Step to R side with R (ct. 1). Step L across in front of R (ct. 2).

14-15 Repeat action of meas. 13 two times (3 in all).

16 Small step R to R side with accent (ct. 1). Hold (ct. 2).

17-32 Repeat action of meas. 1-16 but start stepping on L and extending R.

Figure II

1   Step on R side with R (cts. 1, 2).

2   Step L across and in front of R (ct. 1, 2).

3   Step to R side with R (ct. 1). Step L in back of R (ct. 2).

4   Repeat action of meas. 3 (Fig. II).

5-12   Repeat action of meas. 1-4 (Fig. II) two times (3 in all).

13   Stamp R (ct. 1). Extend L fwd., knee straight and ft. a few inches off floor (ct. 2).

14   Bend L knee so L ft. is under body.

15   Step L next to R (ct. 1). Step R in place (ct. 2).

16   Step L in place (ct. 1). Hold ct. 2.

17-32 Repeat action of meas. 1-16 (Fig. II).
       Repeat action of Fig. I and II 2 more times (3 times complete).
       End by repeating Fig. I again.

SARBA

SOURCE: This Sarba comes from western Rumania in the Banat region.

MUSIC: Record — Rumania and the Gypsies — Bruno 50058, Side A, Band 7 De Tre Potcauii Calul. 2/4 time.

FORMATION: Broken circle of M and W. Leader at R end. Joined hands are held down.

STEPS: Walking steps are done with small plié or bend of knee.

PATTERN

Measures

5   Introduction. No action.

Figure I. Walking

1-9   Starting with R to R, walk 9 steps (1 to a meas.).

10-18   Starting with L to L, walk 9 steps.

Figure II. Moving to Side

1   Facing ctr., step to R side with R (ct. 1). Step L in back of R (ct. 2).

2-6   Repeat action of meas. 1 five more times (6 in all). On meas. 6, ct. 2 stamp L next to R (no wt.).

7-12   Repeat action of meas. 1-6 but start with L and go to L. On meas. 12, ct. 2 stamp R next to L (no wt.).

13-24   Repeat action of Fig. II, meas. 1-12.

25   Stamp R again (no wt.).
Repeat all of Fig. I and Fig. II. Omit meas. 25 of Fig. II. End with wt. on R.

Figure III. Stamps

1-4   Facing ctr., stamp L in front of R (no wt.), bending L knee and pointing L toe to R (meas. 1). Place L next to R (no wt.) (meas. 2). Repeat action for meas. 3-4 but place wt. on L in meas. 4.

5-6   Step to R side with R (meas. 5, ct. 1). Step L in front of R (ct. 2). Step to R side with R (meas. 6, ct. 1). Step L next to R (ct. 2).

7-12   Repeat action of meas. 1-6 (Fig. III) but begin with stamp with R, and do sidestep to L.

13-24   Repeat action of meas. 1-12 (Fig. III). On meas. 24, ct. 2 do not put wt. on R.

Figure IV. Step-Hop Grapevine

1-4   Travelling in CCW direction, step to R on R (meas. 1, ct. 1). Hope on R (ct. 2). Step-hop on L in front of R (meas. 2). Step-hop on R to R (meas. 3). Step-hop on L behind R (meas. 4). (This pattern is like a grapevine step done with step-hops.)

5-32   Repeat action of meas. 1-4 (Fig. IV) 7 more times. On meas. 32, instead of step-hop on L, step L next to R (no wt.).

Figure V. Stamps

1-12   Repeat action of Fig. III, meas. 1-12. This is ½ the original figure so stamps will only be done with the L and R ft. once each and not repeated. End with wt. on L and R free.

Figure VI. Step-Hop Grapevine

1-16   Repeat action of Fig. IV, meas. 1-4 times.

CALUSH DANCE FROM GORJ
(Cah loosh dance from gore yeh)

SOURCE: Calush Dance from Gorj is descended from a traditional religious dance. It is for men only. It was learned by Anatol Joukowsky from the natives in Rumania.

MUSIC: Record — Through Rumania in Song and Dance BR 50155 Side B, Band 3, 4/4 meter. No introduction.

FORMATION: Circle of M with hands on upper arms of neighbors. Stand with ft. astride, facing ctr.

PATTERN

Measures

Figure I

1   Shift wt. onto R with bend of R knee (ct. 1). Ball of

L ft. remains on floor. Bend R knee 3 more times (cts. 2, 3, 4).

2   Shift wt. onto L with bend of L knee (ct. 1). Ball of R ft. remains on floor. Bend L knee 3 more times (cts. 2, 3, 4).

3-8   Repeat action of meas. 1-2 three more times (8 wt. shifts in all).

Figure II

1-3   Let hands move down and join hands with neighbors in a circle. Walk in LOD 6 steps beg. R (each step takes 2 cts.). Small bend of knees on each step.

4   Stamp R (no wt.) (cts. 1, 2). Repeat (cts. 3, 4). On each stamp raise joined hands overhead as an accent.

5-8   Repeat action of meas. 1-4 (Fig. II) but on stamps thrust joined hands down.

9-16   Repeat action of meas. 1-8 (Fig. II).

Variation of Dance
Figure I

1   Keep hands joined and held down as in Fig. II. Ft. again in stride pos. Shift wt. onto R with bend of knee (ct. 1). Ball of L ft. remains on floor. Bend R knee once more (ct. 2). Shift wt. onto L with bend of L knee (ct. 2). Ball of right ft. remains on floor. Bend L knee once more (ct. 4).

2-8   Repeat action of meas. 1 (Fig. I Var.) 7 times (16 wt. shifts in all).

Figure II

1-16   Repeat action of Fig. II.

BREAK IN MUSIC

Figure III

1   Hands are still joined. Facing ctr., take small leap onto R. At same time, sharply bend L knee so L ft.

comes up under body and L heel kicks self (ct. 1). Hop on R and extend L ft. (toe pointed) fwd. sharply by straightening L knee (ct. 2). Small leap onto L beside R, sharply bending R knee so R ft. comes up under body and R heel kicks self (ct. 2). Hop on L and extend R ft. (toe pointed) fwd. sharply by straightening R knee (ct. 2).

2-4   Repeat action of meas. 1 (Fig. III) 3 times (8 in all).

5-8   Release joined hands. Extend arms out a little above shoulder height, elbows straight. Using same ftwk. as in meas. 1-4 (Fig. III) turn once around to R. At end of turn place hands on upper arms of neighbors.

Figure IV

1   Turn body a little R to move in LOD. Step R in LOD (ct. 1). Chug fwd. on R while stretching L leg in LOD (ct. 2). Land on L (ct. 3). Hop on L (ct. 4).

2-8   Repeat action of meas. 1 (Fig. IV) 7 more times (8 in all). At end, hands move from shoulder down to joined pos.

1-8   *Repeat Action of Fig. III.*

1-8   *Repeat Action of Fig. IV.*

1-8   *Repeat Action of Fig. III.*

CHAPTER SIX

CZECHOSLOVAKIA

Czechoslovakia is divided into three parts. In the north is Bohemia, in the middle Moravia and in the southeastern part is Slovakia. When the author was the Vienna Opera House choreographer he had many opportunities to visit Slovakia. It was the first place where we had a chance to study ethnic dance in intact form. The southwestern slopes of the Carpathian mountains and the Danube River lead to Bratislava, the capitol city of Slovakia. North and northwest from Bratislava in the neighboring villages one can find very nice traditional dances. The mountain people preserve the treasures of dance.

In Slovakian folklore the important dance form is the *Couples Dance*. The Szardash (Czardas), an Hungarian dance was adopted by the Slovaks but changed considerably. The music they use is typically Slavic and the steps are more vigorous and free than in the Hungarian version. Each village has its own interpretation as we have seen in the discussions of dances from other countries. Every tune has its special approach by the dancers. In the mountain region of Visoke Tatri there are Slovak mountaineers who dance in a kind of moccasin. They do not wear typical boots.

In the region of Chichmani the dancers wear a costume called Chichmanski Kroj which is unique in all of Europe. It is a brightly colored beautifully embroidered costume. Going down into the valleys like Horehronsko or Dolnehronsko by the Hron River one can see another form of "Czardas Z Kozickyh Ham-

rov." The Nitrianski Tanz presented here is still another Czardas. The third one, "Zahraite Me" means "Gypsy Play For
Me." All are different in their patterns yet each is Slavic and
represents this very particular temperament. This set of Slovak
dances was learned before changes were made in them, and are
presented for the first time in the United States in published
form. We hope they will be preserved.

In the search for new material one day in the Opera House
of Brno in Moravia, the author became re-acquainted with the
choreographer, a ballet master named Vania Psota. He was a
long-time solo dancer in the original Ballet Russe. Many years
before we had worked together. He is now gone, but he provided a great impetus to building ethnic dance for the stage. He

researched primarily in ethnic dance in Czechoslovakia and he has left much fine material for those of us who have followed him.

The music for Slovakian dances, except in the high mountain regions, is very close to symphonic music. It is not as good as it would be if it were really ethnic. Up toward the northern part of Czechoslovakia the music is even more of a disaster. In each Bohemian village there is a little band made up of not quite enough instrumentalists to give a true symphonic sound. But — because all Czechs, Slovaks, and Moravs are good musicians, the music is good. Think what it would be like if the musicians were not talented! In Slovakian Tatri the rustic flute, the shepherd's clarinet and other native instruments provide the clear accompaniment that is truly ethnic. The cimbalo is an Hungarian instrument adopted in Slovakia. This is a fine instrument for use in ethnic dance. Then the Gypsies with their violins producing soft, lyric music take the dancer's heart and he becomes a blind follower of the tune of the violin.

The Slovak State ensemble today presents the folklore of Slovakia. These people are trying to preserve for posterity what is left of the old culture of the mountainous Slovaks.

VRTIELKA
(Vrr-tiel-kah)
(Turning Dance)

SOURCE: This Slovak Czardas, from Nove Zamki, was presented at the 1955 College of the Pacific Folk Dance Camp by Anatol Joukowsky, who learned it while on tour in Slovakia, 1935-36.

MUSIC: Record — Kolo Fextival KF 803-B. Music 2/4, 4/8.

FORMATION: Couples, spaced freely about the floor; ptrs. facing, in ballroom pos. (M L — W R well extended) with M R at W waist. M face LOD.

STEPS: Czardas, Bokazo, Pivot. *Note:* Throughout dance,
                  bend knees on each closing step of Czardas and
                  on Bokazo.

PATTERN

Measures

2/4   *Figure I. Sideward Czardas and Bokazo*
1   *M:* Step R to R (ct. 1), close L to R, bending knees
         (ct. &) step R to R (ct. 2), close L to R, bending
         knees and keeping wt. on R (ct. &).

2   Step L to L (ct. 1), close R to L, bending knees (ct.
         &), step L to L (ct. 2), close R to L, bending knees
         and taking wt. on R (ct. &).

3   Bending both knees, turn L heel diagonally outward
         and close (ct. 1), turn R heel diagonally outward and
         close (ct. &), turn both heels out and quickly close
         (ct. 2), hold (ct. &). *W:* Dance counterpart through-
         out action of meas. 1-3.

4-6   Repeat action of meas. 1-3.
         Figure II. Czardas and Woman Pivot
         Ballroom pos., as described above. M dance directly
         fwd. and bwd. in this fig.

1   M step R fwd. (ct. 1), close L instep to R heel (ct. &),
         step R fwd. (ct. 2), close L instep to R heel (ct. &).
         W step bwd. L (ct. 1), close R heel to L instep (ct. &),
         step bwd. L (ct. 2), close R heel to L instep keeping
         wt. on L (ct. &).

2   M step in place L, R, L (cts. 1 & 2), hold (ct. &); W
         pivot on R CW (one complete turn) under their
         joined hands (ML-WR) (ct. 1), step L in place (ct.
         &), close R to L (ct. 2), hold (ct. &).

3-4   Repeat action of Fig. II, meas. 1-2, M starting bwd.

L, W fwd. R. (W end meas. 3 with wt. on L to prepare for pivot.)

5-7   Repeat action of Fig. 1, meas. 1-3.

Figure III. Diamond With Turn
Hands on hips, ptrs. facing.

1   Both step fwd. diagonally R, R shoulder leading
(passing ptr. face to face) (ct. 1), close L to R (ct. &),
step diagonally R (ct. 2), close L to R (ct. &).

2   Pivoting 1/4 turn R (CW), both step L to L, continuing the diagonal pattern with L shoulder leading (back twd. ptr.) (ct. 1) close R to L (ct. &), step
L to L (ct. 2), close R to L, keeping wt. on L (ct. &).

3   Both turn CW in place to face ptr. (½ turn) stepping R L R (cts. 1 & 2), hold (ct. &).
Note: Action of Fig. II, meas. 1-3 completes half of
the diamond fig., ptrs. having changed places.

4-6   Repeat action of Fig. III, meas. 1-3, to finish in
original place. M end with wt. on L.

Figure IV. Czardas and Woman Pivot
1-7   Repeat action of Fig. II, meas. 1-7.

Figure V. Diamond With Turn
1-6   Repeat action of Fig. III, meas. 1-6.

Figure VI. Czardas and Woman Pivot
1-7   Repeat action of Fig. II, meas. 1-7. On meas. 7, W
steps L R L making ½ turn CW to end at ptr.'s R
side, both facing same direction. Assume open pos.
FAST PART

4/8   *Figure VII. Open Czardas and Woman Cross-Over*
1   Open pos., outside hands on hips. Both step L to L
(ct. 1), close R to L (ct. 2), step L to L (ct. 3), close
R to L (ct. 4).

2   Both starting R and moving R, repeat action of Fig.
        VII, meas. 1.

3   M step in place L R L (cts. 1, 2, 3), hold (ct. 4), while
        W turns CCW (L) in front of M, stepping L R L
        (cts. 1, 2, 3) to end at M L side, (R arm on his L
        shoulder in open pos.) hold (ct. 4). M should assist
        W in cross-over.

4-6   Starting R and moving to R, repeat action of Fig.
        VII, meas. 1-3. W end on M R side on open pos. for
        next fig.

        Figure VIII. Crosshold With Couple Turn

1   M take W L hand from his shoulder with his L, her
        R with his R (L over R, chest high) as both step fwd.
        R (ct. 1), close L to R (ct. 2), step fwd. R (ct. 3), close
        L to R (ct. 4). W keep wt. on R.

2   M step in place R L R, making ½ turn R (CW)
        while he turns W 1½ turns CCW under their raised
        joined hands (cts. 1, 2, 3), hold (ct. 4). W pivot CCW
        stepping L R, close L, keeping wt. on R (cts. 1, 2, 3),
        hold (ct. 4).
        Note: At end of meas. 2, W is on M L, hands joined
        R over L, ptrs. with backs to original direction of
        Fig. VIII.

3   Both step L fwd. (ct. 1), close R to L (ct. 2), step L
        fwd. (ct. 3), close R to L (ct. 4). W keep wt. on L.

4   M step in place L R L, making ½ turn CCW while
        he turns W 1½ turns CW under their raised joined
        hands (cts. 1, 2, 3), hold (ct. 4), W pivots CW, step-
        ping R L; close R, keeping wt. on L (cts. 1, 2, 3) hold
        (ct. 4). End in open pos., facing original direction of
        Fig. VIII.

5-7   In open pos., both starting R, repeat action as de-
        scribed for M in Fig. I, meas. 1-3.

26 meas.   Repeat action of following figures in sequence: Fig.
            VII, VIII, VII, VIII.

            Turn and Pose
            R hands joined, M turn W L (CCW), completing 1
            turn under his R arm. As second turn is started,
            joined R are lowered to end at W R waist as M
            draws her to him in pose.

CZARDAS Z KOSICKYCH HAMROV
(Czardas from Ko zich'ke Ham'rehv)

SOURCE: The Slovakians have borrowed the Hungarian
            Czardas and given it a flavor of their own. This
            particular Czardas has been danced by the Slovak
            Company in Bratislava.

MUSIC: Record — Volkstanz V-7801Z. No introduction.

FORMATION: Double circle, M on inside, facing LOD (CCW).
            M R arm around W, holding W RH at her waist.
            M LH on hip. W L on M R shoulder.

STEPS: *Czardas:* Step to R with R (ct. 1). Close L to R,
            bending knees (ct. 2). Step to R with R (ct. 3).
            Close L to R, wt. still on R (ct. 4). Next step
            would start to L with L. Close ft. together; this
            usually results in a heel click if the shoes and the
            mood of the dancer permit. The M particularly
            like to click their heels.
            Description is same for M and W unless otherwise
            noted.

PATTERN

Measures

4/4 tempo No introduction.

            Figure I
            Step diag. fwd. R with R (ct. 1). Close L to R, bend-
            ing knees (ct. 2). Repeat for cts. 3-4.

2   Walk in LOD 4 steps starting R.

3-4   Repeat action of meas. 1-2.

5-6   Czardas step to R and L.

7   Step to R with R (ct. 1). Close L to R, bending knees (no wt.) (ct. 2). Step to L with L (ct. 3). Close R to L, bending knees (no wt.) (ct. 4).

8   M: Step to R with R (ct. 1). Close L to R (ct. 2). Step R in place (ct. 3). Hold (ct. 4).
         W: With 3 steps (R L R) turn out to R, go behind M and end on L side of him. Close L to R (no wt.) (ct. 4). M puts L arm around W, holding W LH at her waist. M RH on hip. W R on M L shoulder.

9-11   Beginning L instead of R, repeat action of meas. 5-7.

12   M: With 2 steps (L R) make ½ turn R to face RLOD. Close ft. together (ct. 3). Hold (ct. 4). Release W Hs.
         W: With 3 steps (L R L) turn out to L and end facing M. Close R to L (no wt.) (ct. 4). Cpls. are in single circle, M facing RLOD, W LOD. Hs. on hips.

         Figure II (Vocal)
1   Czardas to R.

2   Bokazo: With little hop on R, cross L in front of R (ct. 1). Touch L out to L side (ct. 2). Close ft. together (ct. 3). Hold (ct. 4).

3-4   Repeat action of meas. 1-2 to L. Bokazo done with hop on L and crossing R.

5   Join RH, shoulder level (elbow also shoulder level). L still on hips. Step R, taking a ¼ turn to L so M R side is to R LOD and W R side is to LOD (ct. 1). Close L to R (ct. 2). Step to R with R (ct. 3). Touch L behind R, bending knees (ct. 4). After ¼ turn on ct. 1, M has bk. to ctr. of circle, W faces ctr. Ptrs. are facing.

6   Release RH. Make ½ turn R on 2 steps thusly: Step bkwd. on L twd. original pos. (ct. 1). Step R, completing ½ turn R (ct. 2). Close ft. together and place LH on ptr. L forearm, RH on hip (ct. 3). Hold (ct. 4).

Note: Original pos. refers to place where dancer stood at end of meas. 4.

7   Change places on meas. 7-8. Moving fwd. to ptrs. place, step L (ct. 1). Close R to L, bending knees (ct. 2). Step fwd. L (ct. 3). Close R to L, bending knees (ct. 4).

8   Walk L R (ct. 1-2) into ptrs. place. Close ft. together (ct. 3). Hold (ct. 4). End single circle, W facing ctrs., M bk. to ctr. RH on hips. L on ptrs. L forearm.

9   Step to L on L (ct. 1). Close R to L (ct. 2). Step to L on L (ct. 3). Touch R behind L, with bend of knees (ct. 4). Elbows bend to enable ptrs. to face each other after ct. 1. This pattern is similar to meas. 5.

10   Release LH. Make ½ turn L on 2 steps thusly: Step bkwd. on R twd. original pos. (ct. 1). Step L, completing ½ turn L (ct. 2). Close ft. together and place RH on ptrs. R forearm, LH on hip (ct. 3). Hold (ct. 4). Cpls. now in single circle, M facing ctr., W with bk. to ctr.

Note: Original pos. refers to place where dancer stood at end of meas. 8.

11-12   Changing places, repeat action of meas. 7-8 but starting with R. End single circle, ptrs. facing, M looking RLOD. Hs. on hips.

13-24   Repeat action of meas. 1-12. On meas. 24, W makes ½ turn R to face RLOD. Cpls. in single circle facing RLOD, M behind W. W Hs. on hips, M Hs. on W shoulders.

Figure III

1   Step fwd. R (ct. 1). Hop R (ct. 2). L ft. is crossed behind R about mid-calf on hop. Step fwd. L (ct. 3). Hop L (ct. 4). R ft. crosses behind L leg.

2   4 light runs in RLOD (R L R L).

3-4 Repeat action of meas. 1-2.

5   Step to R side with R (ct. 1). Close L to R, bending knees (ct. 2). Step to R with R (ct. 3). Touch L behind R, bending knees (ct. 4).

6   M: Step L R (cts. 1-2). Close ft. together (ct. 3). Hold (ct. 4). M starts W into her turn and then removes Hs. from her shoulders.
     W: Make 1 turn R in front of M. Step L R (cts. 1-2). Close ft. together (ct. 3). Hold (ct. 4). M puts Hs. bk. on W shoulders at end of turn.

7-8 Repeat action of meas. 5-6 but moving to L with L. W turns L.

9-10 Repeat action of meas. 5-6 exactly except that W makes only ½ turn and ends facing ptr. Both place Hs. on ptrs. shoulders.

11   Step to M L with L (W R) (ct. 1). M close R to L (no wt.), bending knees (ct. 2). W close L to R. Repeat to M R (W L) (cts. 3-4).

12   M shifts Hs. to W waist. Prepare to lift W (ct. 1). Lift W (ct. 2). Put W dn. (cts. 3-4). End Hs. on hips, single circle, ptrs. facing (M facing RLOD).

Figure IV (Vocal)

1-5 Repeat action of Fig. II meas. 1-5.

6   M turns W to L 1½ times under joined RHs. Both step L R L (cts. 1, 2, 3). Hold (ct. 4). M dances in place. W ends at M R side. M holds W RH at her waist with his R H. L H on hips. Cpls. facing RLOD.

7   Czardas step to L.

8   Click heels 3 times. Hold (ct. 4).

9   Step to L with L (ct. 1). Close R to L, bending knees (ct. 2). Step L with L (ct. 3). Touch R behind L, bending knees (ct. 4).

10   With joined RH M turns W to R. W make 1 turn. Both step R L (cts. 1-2). Close ft. together (ct. 3). Hold (ct. 4). W stops at MR but a little behind M. Hold joined RH at shoulder height with M R arm outstretched in front of W. W R arm bent, elbow shoulder height. W L on M R shoulder. M L on hip.

11   Moving RLOD, step R (ct. 1). Close L to R, bending knees (ct. 2). Repeat (cts. 3-4).

12   M makes ½ turn R to face W. W dances in place. Both step R L (cts. 1-2). Close ft. together (ct. 3). Hold (ct. 4). End single circle, M facing LOD. W facing M. Hs. on hips.

13-23 Repeat action of meas. 1-11 exactly. After meas. 17 ptrs. will be facing LOD.
       In meas. 22 movement is LOD.

24   Repeat meas. 12 exactly but W also makes ½ turn R to end with bk. to M. Cpls. in single circle facing RLOD. M H on W shoulders, W Hs. on hips.

Figure III (repeated)

1-12 Repeat action of Fig. III. Dance ends with M lifting W.

DETVA CZARDAS

SOURCE: Detva Czardas comes from the Detva Valley in Slovakia. It was learned by Anatol Joukowsky in Bratislava in 1938.

MUSIC: Record — Czardas from Detva 45 rpm. Special re-
                    cording. Dance is in 4/4 and 2/4 meter. Intro.
                    and 1st part have no meter.

FORMATION: Can be done by cpls. or one M and 2 W. Either
                    way, M is in inside circle with back to ctr. W are
                    in outer circle facing their ptr. M join hands in
                    their circle and W do same in their circle.

STEPS: *Double Czardas:* Step to R with R (ct. 1). Close
                    L to R, bending knees (ct. 2). Step to R with R
                    (ct. 3). Close L to R, bending knees (no wt.) (ct.
                    4). Next step would start to L with L.

PATTERN

Measures

no meter   Introduction. This is instrumental. Stand in place.

            Figure I. Walking
            There is still no meter structure so reference will be
            made to the musical phrase.

Phrase I   Circles walk to own R.

Phrase II   Circles walk to own L. Ptrs. are again opp.

Phrase III M offers R arm to ptr. If M has 2 W, he steps be-
            tween them and offers both an arm. All walk CCW
            and wheel CCW at end of phrase.

Phrase IV   All walk CW. At end of phrase, M turn ¼ R to
            face ctr. W step to inside to face ptr. with back to
            ctr. If in cpls., assume shoulder-waist pos. If a trio,
            make small circle by grasping adjacent forearms.

4/4 meter   *Figure II. Czardas, Clicks and Walk*
    1-2   Double Czardas to own R and L.

    3   Beg. R, 1 Double Czardas, moving twd. ctr. M go
            fwd. W back up.

4   Moving away from ctr., step R (ct. 1), L (ct. 2), close R to L (ct. 3). Hold ct. 4.

5   Moving to own R, step R (ct. 1). Cross L behind R (ct. 2). With a little jump, take stride pos. (ct. 3). Click heels together (ct. 4).

6   Repeat action of meas. 5 but start with L and move to L.

7-10   Repeat action of meas. 5-6 two more times.

11-12   Beg. L, circle CW with 7 walking steps. End with click of heels. No. of circles is up to cpl. or trio but try to end where you began.

Figure III. Walking

Phrase V   M again offers arm to W and repeat action of Phrase
Phrase VI   III and IV. End in a single circle, W to R of ptr. If a trio, M is between his W. All hands joined.

There is now a break and a change in the music.

2/4 meter   *Figure IV. Circling CCW*

1   Step to L side on ball of L ft. (ct. 1). Step flat on R in front of L, bending knees (ct. 2).

2-4   Repeat action of meas. 1 (Fig. IV) three more times (4 in all).

5-6   Beg. L, take 4 running steps CW.

7-18   Repeat action of meas. 1-6 (Fig. IV) two more times.

Figure V. Kick Step

1   Step on R, bending L knee so L ft. is under body (ct. 1). With a little hop, extend L straight fwd. or a little in front of R (ct. 2).

2   Repeat action of meas. 1 (Fig. V) but step on L and bend R knee.

3-4   Repeat action of meas. 1-2 (Fig. V).

5   Moving away from ctr., step R (ct. 1), L (ct. 2).

6   Close R to L (ct. 1). Hold ct. 2.

7-12   Repeat action of meas. 1-6 (Fig. V) but on meas. 11-12 move twd. the ctr.

13-36   Repeat action of meas. 1-12 (Fig. V) two more times.

Figure VI. Circling CCW

1-18   Repeat action of Fig. IV except on the last 4 running steps (meas. 17-18) M bring W in twds. ctr. to take same pos. as at end of Prase IV (W have backs to ctr.). Both cpls. and trios take forearm hold.

Figure VII. Kick Step

1-24   Repeat action of Fig. V meas. 1-24 with one adjustment. On meas. 5-6 M moves away from ctr. so W must move fwd. When M moves fwd., W back up. Cross kicking ft. over supporting ft. as much as is necessary to avoid kicking others.

25-35   Repeat action of Fig. IV, meas. 1 eleven times. Cpls. may change to shoulder-waist pos.

36   Jump to stride pos. (ct. 1) Click heels (ct. 2).

TINGI LINGI

SOURCE: Tingi Lingi is a Moravian couple dance and a progressive one.

MUSIC: Record — Folk Art. FALP-I, side 1, Tingi Lingi Boom. 2/4 time.

FORMATION: Double circle, ptrs. facing, M back to ctr. M hands just behind hips with palms out. W hands on hips, fingers fwd. Movement of circle is always CW.

STEPS: *Basic Step:* Step to R on R side (ct. 1). Close L to R with bend of knees (ct. 2). Next step would again start on R. Step may be started on L and would continue on L.

Hand Hold (used on turns): With elbows bent, join R hands with ptr. at shoulder level. Join hands palm to palm with base of fingers at R angles to base of ptrs. fingers. Free hand remains on hip (W) or just behind hip (M).

PATTERN

Measures

2/4 time   No introduction.

1-4   Dance 4 basic steps moving CW. M starts R, W L.

5-6   Join R hands and change places (½ circle CW). M walks R, L, R, close L to R (no wt.). W starts walk with L.

7-10   Repeat action of meas. 1-4 but M start L, W R (M is on outside).

11-12   Join R hands and change places (½ circle CW). M walks L, R, L, close R to L (no wt.). W starts walk with R.

13-16   Repeat action of meas. 1-4.

17-19   Joining R hands, make 1 CW circle on 6 steps. M starts R, W L.

20-23   Repeat action of meas. 1-4.

24-25   On 2 basic steps, starting R, M moves to R to end in front of next W. Original W ptr. also dances 2 basic steps (starting L), and moves to her L but takes smaller steps to allow M to progress.

26-29   Repeat action of meas. 1-4, facing new ptr.

30-32   Joining R hands, make 1 CW circle on 6 steps. M starts R, W L.

33-36   Repeat action of meas. 1-4.

37-28   Repeat progression figure of meas. 24-25.
             Repeat dance from beginning 4 times (5 in all).

3 chords   Ending: Bow to ptr.
             M: Step to R on R (chord 1). Close L to R and bow
             from waist (chord 2). Recover from bow (chord 3).
             W: Step to L on L (chord 1). Placing R behind L
             curtsey to ptr. (chord 2). Recover from curtsey
             (chord 3).

A JA TZO SARITSA
(Ah Yah Tso Sah reet sah)
(I Am Like A Queen)

SOURCE: A Ja Tzo Saritsa is a Moravian couple dance that
               takes its name from the first words of the song
               that is sung.

MUSIC: Record — Folk Art, FALP-I, side 2, band 2. A Ja
               Tzo Saritsa 2/4 & 3/4 time.

FORMATION: Lines of 5 or 6 cpls., ptrs. facing, M back to mu-
               sic. M join hands in line, W same. Free hands of
               end M just behind hip, palms out. End W hands
               on hips, fingers fwd. Lines about 6 ft. apart.

STEPS: *Couple Turn:* Take modified shoulder waist pos.
               (W L and M R hands joined, palm to palm, and
               held on W L hip. W R hand on M L shoulder.
               M L hand on W R forearm). Step fwd. on R and
               bend knee slightly (ct. 1). Bring L ft. to R heel,
               taking wt. on ball of L (ct. &). Repeat action for
               cts. 2, &. Usually takes 1 meas. to make 1 full
               turn CW.

PATTERN

Measures

3/4 time   No introduction.

Figure I. Passive Pattern (Both Lines)

1   Turning to face R, walk R, L, R. (All walking steps in Passive Pattern take 1 ct.).

2   Making ½ turn to L, walk L, R, L.

3   Making ¼ turn R to face ptr., walk fwd. R, L, R. On last step on R, bend knee.

4   Walk bkwd. to place, L, R, L.

5-12   Repeat action of meas. 1-4 (Fig. 1) twice (3 in all).

Figure II. Woman's Active Pattern (Vocal)

1   Woman: Walking diag. fwd. R twd. M line, step R (ct. 1), L (ct. 2), R (ct. 3), stamp L next to R (no wt.) (ct. &). As L is brought fwd. to be stepped on (ct. 2), bend R knee a little. Hands on hips, fingers fwd.

2   Walking diag. fwd. L twd. M line, repeat action of meas. 1 (Fig. II) but start with L.

3   Moving slightly fwd. twd. M line, step R (ct. 1), L (ct. &), R (ct. 2). Stamp L next to R (no wt.) (ct. 3). As L is stamped, strike bottom of R fist against top of L fist as if to say, "I want my way."

4   Make ½ turn to R, stepping L, R, L (cts. 1 & 2). Hands are returned to hips and W back is to M. No action rest of meas.

5-8   Starting with back to M, repeat action of meas. 1-4 (Fig. II). W will move away from M line. After ½ turn R on meas. 8, W will again face M.

9-12   Repeat action of meas. 1-4 (Fig. II). W end with back to M.

Man: During 12 meas. of W Active Pattern, continue Passive Pattern (Fig. I), dancing it 3 more times.

Figure III. Man's Active Pattern

1   Man: With hands just behind hips, walk diag. fwd. R twd. W line, stepping R (ct. 1), L (ct. 2), R (ct. 3). Slap outside of L heel with L hand (ct. &). On the slap the L ft. is brought up behind to knee level.

2   Walking diag. fwd. L twd. W line, repeat action of meas. 1 (Fig. III) but start with L. Slap R heel with R.

3   Moving slightly fwd. twd. W line, step R (ct. 1). Close L to R, bending knees in preparation for a jump (ct. 2). Jump into air, spreading legs apart sdwd. (ct. &). Land ft. together (ct. 3).

4   Make ½ turn R, stepping L, R, L (cts. 1, & 2). On each step clap back of R hand against palm of L as if to say, "Why must that be so?" Hands are returned to pos. and M back is to W. No action for rest of meas.

5-8   Starting with back to W, repeat action of meas. 1-4 (Fig. III). M will move away from W line. After ½ turn R on meas. 8, M will again face W.

9-12   Repeat action of meas. 1-4 (Fig. III). M ends with back to W.

Woman: On meas. 1-2, walk 6 steps (starting R with back to M) to beginning pos. Hands are on hips. On meas. 3-4 turn R to face M line and join hands. On meas. 5-12 dance Passive Pattern (Fig. I meas. 1-4) two times.

Figure IV. Woman's Active Pattern (Vocal)

1-12   Woman: Repeat action of Fig. II.

Man: On meas. 1-2 walk 6 steps (starting R with back to W) to beginning pos. Hands just behind hips. On meas. 3-4 turn R to face W line and rejoin hands. On meas. 5-12 dance Passive Pattern (Fig. I meas. 1-4) two times.

Figure V. Man's Active Pattern

1-10   M and W repeat action of Fig. III meas. 1-10 as given for each.

11-12   M make R turn and walk (2 steps to a ct.) to ptr. Join hands with ptr. Cpls. at both ends of line curve around so as to form a double circle, ptrs. facing, M back to ctr. All cpls. adjust a little to help form circle.

2/4 time   *Figure VI. Couple Turn and Progress*
1-2   Take modified shoulder waist pos. as described and make 2 CW turns with ptr.

3   Using joined hands (M R, W L) for lead, M turn W ½ turn R. Both step R, L, R (cts. 1, &, 2). Hold ct. &. Do not drop joined hands. Ptrs. end side by side, W to R of M. Free hands on hips or at sides.

4   Both stepping L, R, L (cts. 1, &, 2) M turn W one full turn L to again end side by side, W to R of M. Joined hands now encircle W waist. Hold ct. &. Do not catch W R arm at her side.

5   Repeat action of meas. 3 (Fig. VI) but W makes one full turn R. During meas. 3-5 M dances almost in place.

6   Both stepping L, R, L (cts. 1, &, 2) M moves to W on his L. W moves to M on her R (M moves up one place (CCW) in circle.

7-42   Repeat action of meas. 1-6 (Fig. VI) six more times (7 in all). On meas. 42 do not progress to new ptr. Instead repeat action of meas. 4 (Fig. VI).

ZAHRAJCE MI
(Zah rhi tay Me)
(Play to Me)

SOURCE: Zahrajce Mi takes its name from the song title meaning "Play To Me." Since Slovakia is near the Hungarian border the steps and music show a Hungarian influence.

MUSIC: Record — Volkstans. V-7801. Zahrajce Mi. 2/4 time. No introduction.

FORMATION: This is best danced by groups of 4 to 8 cpls. At start of dance ptrs. are facing with M back to music. Cpls. are in no specific formation but it should be remembered that in Fig. III cpls. will form a single circle. It might be well to first join hands in a circle and then assume beginning pos. M hands are at back, waist level, palms out. W hands are on hips, fingers fwd. Whenever one or both hands are free, these pos. are used.

PATTERN

Measures

Figure I

1   Moving to own R, step R (ct. 1). Close L to R (ct. 2).

2   Repeat action of meas. 1.

3   Click heels twice (cts. 1-2).

4-6   Repeat action of meas. 1-3 but move L with L.

7   Step on R twd. ptr. (ct. 1). Close L to R (ct. 2).

8   Joining R hands, repeat action of meas. 7.

9   M turns W to her L (CCW) under joined hands 1½ times. W ends at M R side, R hands joined and held at W R hip. W L hand on hip. M L hand just be-

hind waist. M back to music still. W step R, L, R (cts. 1 & 2) on turn, M clicks twice while W turns (cts. 1 & 2).

10 Moving to L, step L (ct. 1). Close R to L (ct. 2).

11 Repeat action of meas. 10.

12 Click heels twice (cts. 1, 2).

13-16 Starting with R, walk 8 steps to make 1 CW circle.

17 M turn W to R (CW) 1½ turns to end ptrs. facing in original pos., M back to music. W steps R, L, R, L.

18 Click heels twice (cts. 1, 2).

Figure II (Vocal)

1 Joining R hands, step diag. R on R twd. ptr. (ct. 1). Close L to R (no wt.) (ct. 2).

2 Step back to place on L (ct. 1). Close R to L (no wt.) (ct. 2).

3 Ptrs. change places under joined hands. Take large step R (ct. 1). Step L (ct. 2). Close R beside L (no wt). (ct. &). Each make ½ turn R (CW) and in doing so pass back to back with ptr. End facing ptr. with hands still joined.

4-6 Repeat action of meas. 1-3 exactly to return to place.

7-9 Move R hands up to hold ptr. just above R elbow. R hips adjacent. Moving fwd. (CW) promenade 6 steps starting on R. On steps 1-5 M L hand is held high out to side. On step 6 M brings it down to take R hand of W. W L on hip.

10 Cpls. turn in modified shoulder-waist pos., R hips adjacent. M place W R hand on his L shoulder and hold it there. M R on W waist. W L just above M R elbow. Step on R with bend of knee (ct. 1). Step on ball of L ft. with straight knee (ct. &). Repeat for cts. 2, &.

11-12   Repeat action of meas. 10 twice. Turn has 6 cts. in all. On last ct. & of meas. 12 swing L over R while making ½ turn R to assume promenade pos. of meas. 7-9 but with L hands holding above ptrs. L elbow. Do not step on L until ct. of meas. 13.

13-15   Repeat promenade of meas. 7-9 in CCW direction starting with L, L hips adjacent. M R hand is high until step 6 when M takes L hand of W.

16-18   Repeat action of meas. 10-12 but with L hips adj. M place W L hand on his R shoulder and hold it there. M L on W waist. W R just above M L elbow. Start turn by stepping on L, bending knee.

19-36   Repeat action of meas. 1-18. Cut last 2 cts. of last turn and form circle. Cpls. face ctr., W to R of M. M R on W R hip. W L on M R shoulder. Free hands on hips as described.

Figure III

1   Moving to R, step R (ct. 1). Close L to R (ct. 2).

2   Repeat action of meas. 1.

3   M click heels twice (cts. 1, 2). W turn R once and resume pos. Step R, L, R (cts. 1, 2).

4-6   Repeat action of meas. 1-3 but moving to L with L. Does not turn but clicks same as M.

7-12   Repeat action of meas. 1-6.

13-17   Repeat action of meas. 1-5.

18   Moving out to enlargen circle, step L, R, L (cts. 1 & 2). At same time turn to face ptr. End in single circle, ptrs. facing, M facing LOD (CCW).

Figure IV (Vocal)

1-18   Repeat action of Fig II, meas. 1-18. Only difference is that M faces LOD instead of having back to music. Omit last 2 steps on last turn and reform circle. W to R of M. Hands on upper arms of neighbors.

Figure V

1   Moving to L, step L (ct. 1). Close R to L (ct. 2).

2-3   Repeat action of meas. 1 twice.

4-6   Still moving L (CW) walk 6 steps. Since cpls. are still facing ctr., cross R in front of L.

7   Step to L on ball of L ft., knee straight (ct. 1). Step on R in front of L, bending knee (ct. &). Repeat for cts. 2, &.

8-12   Repeat action of meas. 7 five more times (12 cts. in all). Circle moves rapidly to L.

13-18   Using same ft. pattern as in meas. 7-12, turn with ptr., R hips adj. Arm pos. same as in Fig. II, meas. 10. Finish facing in LOD, double circle, W to R of M. W L on M R shoulder. M holds W R hand at her waist. Free hands on hips as described.

Figure VI (Vocal)

1   Progressing in LOD (CCW) step R (ct. 1). Close L to R (ct. 2).

2   Repeat action of meas. 1.

3   With joined R hands, M turn W to R (CW). W step R (ct. 1), L (ct. &). Step R next to L (no wt.) (ct. 2). W make 1 turn, ending at R of M but a little behind him. M steps R, L, R (no wt.) (cts. 1, 2). Hold joined R hands at shoulder height with M R arm outstretched in front of W. W L on M R shoulder. M L on hip.

4   Continuing in LOD step R (ct. 1). Close L to R (ct. 2).

5   Step R in LOD (ct. 1). Close L to R (ct. 2). W puts no wt. on step L.

6   M starts W into L (CCW) turn by a lead from joined R hands. Dropping joined R hands, M turn ½ R to face RLOD, stepping R, L, R (cts. 1 & 2). W turn 1½ times L (CW) to end facing RLOD at L side of M. W step L (ct. 1), R (ct. &), L (ct. 2), close R to L (ct. &). M L hand holds W L at waist. W R on M L shoulder. M R on hip as described. (Hand holds same as meas. 1 but reversed).

7-9   Moving in RLOD repeat action of meas. 1-3 but start with L. In meas. 9 M will turn W to L.

10-11   Moving in RLOD repeat action of meas. 4-5.

12   M make ¼ turn L to end back to ctr. Step L (ct. 1), R (ct. &), hold (2). W make 1¼ turn R to end facing M. W step R (ct. 1), L (ct. &), R (ct. 2). Hands on hips.

13   Step starts on ct. & of meas. 12. Bending R knee, raise L leg out to side (ct. &). Close L to R straightening R knee (ct. 1). Bending L knee, raise R leg out to side (ct. &). Close R to L, straightening L knee (ct. 2). Bending R knee, raise L leg out to side (ct. &).

14   Close L to R, straightening R knee (ct. 1). Bending L knee, raise R leg out to side (ct. &). Close R to L, straightening L knee (ct. 2). Hold (ct. &).

15   Click heels twice (cts. 1, 2).

16-17   Repeat action of meas. 13-14.

18   Both step L, R L (cts. 1 & 2). M make ¼ turn L to face LOD. W make ¼ turn R to face LOD. Assume hand pos. of meas. 1 (Fig. VI).

19-35   Repeat action of meas. 1-17 (Fig. VI).

36   W click heels twice (cts. 1, 2). M click heels (ct. 1). Raise L lower leg (knee bent) and slap boot with L

hand (ct. &). On rebound of slap, hand stays up. M click heels (ct. 2). Hold (ct. &).

NITRIANSKI TANZ

SOURCE: This is a Slovakian Czardas for one man and two women. Learned by Anatol Joukowsky while in Slovakia.

MUSIC: Record — Fold Art FALP I Side 2, Band 1. Nitrianski Czardas 4/4 and 2/4 meter. No introduction.

FORMATION: Sets of 1 M between 2 W in a large circle all facing ctr. of the large circle. M join hands with outside hands of W in front of W. W inside hands on near should. of M. Joined hands held a little fwd. so all shoulders are in a line.

STEPS: *Walk:* Knees are relaxed.
W Turns: On R turns, start with R ft. On L turns, start with L ft. This means that W may have to anticipate turns to free correct ft. Special directions are given to that 1 W. Description same for M and W unless otherwise noted.

PATTERN

Measures

4/4 meter *Figure I. Facing Ctr.*

1 Step to R on R (cts. 1, 2). Step L over R (cts. 3, 4).

2 Step to R on R (cts. 1, 2). Close L to R (no wt.) (cts. 3, 4).

3-4 Repeat action of meas. 1-2 but start to L with L.

5 Repeat action of meas. 2.

6 Repeat action of meas. 2 but start to L with L. RW take wt. on cts. 3, 4.

7   M and LW small step to R on R (ct. 1). Close L to R
       (ct. 2). LW hold cts. 2, 4. Man may click heels on cts.
       3, 4. RW make L turn on 3 steps beg. L (1 to a ct.).
       Close on ct. 4. Keep hands joined on turn to RW
       ends beside M with M R arm around RW and joined
       R hands on her R hip. Her L hand on M R shoulder.

8   M and RW small step to L on L (ct. 1). Close R to
       L (no wt.) (ct. 2). RW hold cts. 3, 4. M may click
       heels. LW make R turn beg. R on 3 steps (1 to a ct.).
       Close on ct. 4. LW end in same pos. as RW but at
       L side of M.

9   Beg. R, all move twd. ctr. on 4 walks.

10   Click heels on cts. 1 and 3.

11-12 Raising joined hands, M give lead to W for turns.
       RW turn R twice (beg. R) on 8 steps. LW turn L
       twice (beg. L) on 8 steps (no wt. on last). W end in
       beg. pos. of Fig. I. M step in place for 4 cts. and then
       click heels on cts. 1 & 3 of meas. 12. On last ct. end
       ft. together, ready to start dance again.

13-20 Repeat action of meas. 1-8.

21   Beg. R, all back out of ctr. on 4 walks (1 to a ct.).

22   Click Heels on cts. 1 & 3.

23   Keeping hand hold, on 4 steps M turn RW ½ turn
       R and LW ½ turn L. M & RW beg. R. LW beg L.
       RW no wt. on last. W end side by side with backs to
       ctr. and facing M. Hands still joined. W free hands
       on hips, fingers fwd.

24   On 4 steps, M wheel set ¼ turn to his R so M faces
       LOD and W RLOD. M beg. R, W L. Instead of
       walking, M may click heels on cts. 1 & 3.

2/4 meter *Figure II. Facing LOD*

Description for M, W opp.

1   In LOD, step fwd. R (ct. 1), L (ct. 2). (W start bwd. on L).

2   In LOD, step fwd. R (ct. 1), L, bending knee and extending R ft. to side (ct. 2).

3   In place step R (ct. 1), L (ct. &), R, bending knee and extending L ft. to side (ct. 2). Hold ct. &.

4   Repeat action of meas. 3 (Fig. II) but start L.

5-8 Repeat action of meas. 1-4 (Fig. II).

9-10 In LOD, step R (ct. 1), L (ct. 2), R (meas. 10, ct. 1). Close L to R (ct. 2). Thus far W has done opp. Now follow specific directions.

11   M small step to R on R, LW to L on L (ct. 1). M close L to R, LW R to L (both no wt.) (ct. 2). At same time, M turn RW ½ turn L on 2 steps beg. L. RW end at R side of M, joined R hands on her R hip. Her L hand on M R shoulder. This is same pos. for RW as at end of meas. 7, Fig. I.

12   M & RW small step to L on L (ct. 1). Close R to L (no wt.) (ct. 2). At same time, M turn LW ½ turn R on 2 steps beg. R. LW end at L side of M, joined L hands at her hip. Her R hand on M L shoulder. This is the same pose for LW as at end of meas. 8, Fig I. All are now facing LOD.

13-14 Walk 4 steps in LOD, all beg. R. LW no wt. on last step.

15-16 On 3 steps M turn RW ½ turn R (beg. R) and LW ½ turn L (beg. L) so W end in starting pos. of Fig. II. M steps R, L, R (no wt.). All hold ct. 2 of meas. 16.

17-28   Repeat action of meas. 1-12 (Fig. II).

29-30   All beg. R. On 4 steps M wheel set ½ turn to his L so all face ctr. LW on wt. on last step.

31-32   On 3 steps M turn RW 1 turn R (beg. R) and LW 1 turn L (beg. L) so W end in starting pos. of Fig. I. M step R, L, L (no wt.). All hold ct. 2 of meas. 32.

Repeat Action of Figure I

1-24   This time the music is in 2/4 time. Action is just the same as in 4/4 time but cts. differ. Meas. are counted 1, &, 2, & instead of 1, 2, 3, 4. Same no. of steps are taken in each meas. Since tempo is faster, M may wish to release W hands during the turns on meas. 11-12.

1-32   *Repeat Action of Figure II.*

1-24   *Repeat Action of Figure I* (2/4 time).

CHAPTER SEVEN

POLAND

Poland today is one of the countries of Eastern Europe which preserves the folk dance in living form. Dance plays a very important part in community life. From the Baltic Sea in the north to the Carpathian Mountains in the south this large country contains many diverse forms of ethnic dances which, although basically Polish in character, reflect historical and geographical associations with surrounding countries. Russians in the northeast, Ukrainians in the southeast, Southern Slavs and Hungarians in the southwest and the Germans in the west represent the most important influences in the Polish dance. Poland, herself, with her dances rich in expressive spirit and characteristic steps exerts in her turn a very strong influence on the dances of her neighbors. As one example, Scandinavian dances embody many unmistakably Polish steps, forms and names. To the south of Poland and spread throughout the whole of Europe some form of Polka can be found. The origin of this is indisputable.

Like the dances of other countries Polish dances evolved after many centuries. From the first type of Slavic circle dance, religious or ritualistic in origin, the dances have arrived at the graceful, nobly expressive contemporary Mazurkas. The lakes of the Mazurs, the swamp lands of Pinsk, the fertile Wisla plains, and the rugged Carpathian Mountains have all contributed through their geographical characteristics to the dances of their inhabitants.

The best known are the dances of the Gurals of the Carpathian Mountains; memorial dances of the Zbunichki, heroic souvenirs of the insurrections of these people against national

enemies; the whole related group of Krakowiaks named according to the region in which they originated; the Mazurs, the Obereks, the Kujawiaks, of Central Poland, the Contradances and Moruwkas of the north present an interesting study for any serious ethnic dance student.

The traditional respectful attitude of the Polish male toward the woman gives a special spirit to the Polish dance in that the woman's role is not subordinate to the man's, but on the contrary, complements his in perfect harmony.

All the significant events of family and social life are depicted in the dances of Poland. The Polish dances presented in this book are in choreo-arrangement adapted to recorded music. The characteristic ethnic steps are used in the simple basic Krakowiak, the "Pod Borem." This is a Krakowiak for three and is a progressive circle dance with simple steps.

The Polonez is a dance ordinarily done in the city. It is a ceremonial dance, a slow walking variation of Kujawiak, and it shows how the Shilahta or nobles dance. Two Polonezes presented here are one city Polonez from Warszawa, and one from the small village, Beskids.

Many Polish composers such as Frederic Chopin made Polish dance forms famous so they are known all over the world. In an attempt to preserve these Polish dances there have been formed two institutes. The first is the National Institute School of Folk Music and Dance located at Masovia and the second is in Ljubinecz, west Poland. With the establishment of these Institutes perhaps there is no longer danger that the Polish dance will be forgotten.

POD BOREM
(Under Pine)

SOURCE: Pod Borem is a simple version of the Krakowiak, a dance form that originated with the peasants of Krakow.

MUSIC: Record — Bruno BR 50017 Side A, Band 2 "Poland in Song and Dance." 4/4 meter.
Vanguard VRS 6001 or 9016 (At the Edge of the Forest).

FORMATION: Cpls. facing, M back to ctr. Inside hands joined and held shoulder height, elbows bent. M L hand behind back at belt level. W R hand at hip, fingers fwd. Cpls. do not have to be in a formal circle as long as all move in CCW (LOD) direction (as in free-style waltz).

STEPS: *Pas de Basque* (2 to a meas.): Leap swd. on L (ct. 1). Step R ft. in front of L (ct. &). Step in place on L (ct. 2). Hold ct. & but prepare for the next leap which is onto the R. Repeat pas de basque on the R for cts. 3, &, 4.

PATTERN

Measures

3 meas.   Introduction. Start after the 4 chords.

Figure I

1-3   Beg. M L, W R dance 6 pas de basques in place. There will be some "away and together" movement.

Figure II

4   Beg. M L, W R walk 3 steps in LOD, ending in a back-to-back pos. (cts. 1-3). Click free ft. (M R, W L) to supporting ft. (ct. 4). M L hand may be on waist or move freely at side.

5   Beg. M R, W L walk 3 steps in LOD, ending in a face-to face pos. (cts. 1-3). Click free ft. to supporting ft. (ct. 4).

6-7   Repeat action of meas. 4-5. Finish face to face with both hands joined straight across and stretched swd.

8   With wt. on M R, W L hop and click free ft. to supporting ft. 4 times (once on each chord). Move in LOD while clicking. Repeat dance from beginning 5 more times (6 in all). Last repeat has only 3 clicks.

POLONEZ WARSZAWSKI

SOURCE: This polonaise comes from the region of Warsaw, Poland.

MUSIC: Mazowaze Song and Dance Ensemble of Poland. Bruno BR50071 Side B, Band 8 Polonez Warzawski 3/4 time.

FORMATION: Cpls. in double circle facing LOD (CCW), M to L and a little behind W. L hands joined and extended fwd. about shoulder height. W hold skirt with R. M R hand at small of his back, palm out or extended at shoulder level in a protective arc behind W but not touching her. Ptrs. should not be too close to each other.

STEPS: *Basic Step:* Step fwd. R (ct. 1). Step fwd. L (ct. 2). Step fwd. R, bending knee and almost at same time, lightly brush L ft. fwd. (ct. 3). Next step would start fwd. with L. Description same for M and W unless otherwise noted.

PATTERN

Measures

8 Introduction. No action.

1-3 Both starting R, dance 3 basic steps in LOD (starts with vocal).

4 W dance 1 basic step as before but almost in place. Both start L. M backs up twd. ctr. on 1 basic step so as to end with L hands still joined and M almost facing RLOD. W still faces LOD.

5-6 Change places by moving fwd. in an arc, L hands still joined. Dance 1 basic step fwd., starting R, twd. ptrs. place (meas. 5). Continuing fwd. movement, step L (meas. 6, ct. 1), step R (ct. 2), point L toe and shoulder to ptr. (ct. 3). W now on inside of circle facing RLOD. M on outside facing LOD.

7-8 Cross over to take starting pos. of meas. 1 (Promenade), M moving straight over and W turning under joined L hands. Dance 1 basic step starting L. Continuing movement, step R (meas. 8, ct. 1), step L (ct. 2), stamp R next to L (no wt.) (ct. 3). Cpls. are now in pos. to start dance again.

Repeat action of meas. 1-8 to end of music.

POLONEZ FROM BESKIDS

SOURCE: This Polonaise pattern comes from the area of the Beskids Mountains.

MUSIC: Record — Polish Accordian in Hi-Fi Bruno BR 50136 Side B, Band 2.
               Vienna Opera Ball MGM Side 1, Band 1.
               Any evenly phrased Polonaise.

FORMATION: Form a circle of sets of three, 1 M between 2 W. All join hands with arms comfortably outstretched. Release hands between trios and each trio turn to face LOD. M stand a little back of W, with joined hands extended fwd. Arms are parallel to floor. W outside hands hold skirts. Whenever hands are free W hold skirts.

STEPS: *Basic Step:* Step fwd. R (ct. 1). Step fwd. L (ct. 2). Step fwd. R, bending R knee and extending L ft. fwd. (ct. 3). Next step would start fwd. with L.

PATTERN

Measures

3/4 meter   *Figure I*

1-4   Beg. R, dance 4 Basic Steps in LOD.

5   With 1 Basic Step, beg. R, wheel trio ¼ turn CCW to face ctr.

6   Beg. L, dance 1 Basic Step twd. ctr.

7   Beg. R, dance 1 Basic Step in place as M leads W twds. each other so W face M with W back to ctr.

8   Releasing hands, M bows from waist to W. W join near hands and curtsey to M, L ft. going behind. Dancers are now in 2 concentric circles, W on inside facing out and M on outside facing ctr.

9-12   Both circles move to own L. Dance 4 Basic Steps beg. R. W keep her hands joined and free hand holding skirts. M put R hand at small of back, palm out and extend L hand diag. L fwd. Don't count original ptr. and end facing 4th set of W or 4th M.

13   M cross R hand over L and take W hands that were joined hands to face out of ctr. Trios are now in pos. as in meas. 1 but with back to ctr.

14-15   Beg. L, dance 2 Basic Steps moving from ctr.

16   With 1 Basic Step, beg. L, M wheel set $\frac{1}{4}$ turn CCW so M and R W are facing LOD. L W continue $\frac{1}{2}$ turn more in place so as to face RLOD but still on the L side of M (L shoulders will be adjacent). M and L W release hands. M and R W change hands so M L and W L are joined. W hold skirts with free hands and M put R at small of his back.

Figure II

1-8   *M and R W* dance 3 Basic Steps, beg. R, in LOD. On meas. 4 (1 Basic Step) M place R hand at R W waist and wheel $\frac{1}{2}$ turn CCW to face RLOD. Dance W Basic Steps in RLOD. On meas. 8 M lead R W to cross in front and end on outside circle. As R W crosses over, M turn $\frac{1}{2}$ turn CCW (L) to face LOD. L W should now be standing at M L, both facing LOD.
   L W dance 4 Basic Steps, beg. R, in RLOD. Turn R on ct. 3, meas. 4 to face LOD. Return to place with 4 Basic Steps. All L W are moving in an inside circle CW (4 meas.) and CCW (4 meas.).

9-16   M join R hands with L W. M now promenades with L W as R W moves in an outer circle.
   M and L W dance 3 Basic Steps, beg. R, in LOD. On meas. 12 (1 Basic Step) M wheel with LW $\frac{1}{2}$ turn CW to face RLOD. Dance 3 Basic Steps in

RLOD. On meas. 16 M wheel with L W ½ turn CW to face LOD. R W should now be at M R side. *R W* dance 4 Basic Steps, beg. R, in RLOD. Turn R on ct. 3, meas. 12 to face LOD. Return to place on 4 Basic Steps. All R W are moving in an outside circle CW (4 meas.) and CCW (4 meas.). Change to original hand pos. of Fig. I and repeat dance from beginning.

KRAKOWIAK PO TRUIKAM

SOURCE: Krakowiak Po Truikam (True' ee Kahm) trans-lated means "Krakowiak for Three" and is a progressive dance for 1 man and 2 women.

MUSIC: Records — Poland in Song and Dance — Bruno 50017 Side A, Band 10. Music of Poland — Van-guard VRS 6001 Side 1, Band 5.

FORMATION: A large circle of sets of 3. 1 M between 2 W in each set, all facing LOD. M holds inside hands of W, elbows bent, hands at shoulder height. Free hand of W holds skirts.

STEPS: All walking steps are done 2 to a meas.
                Pas de Basque: Low leap onto R (ct. 1). Step L in front of R (ct. &). Step R in place (ct. 2). Hold (ct. &). Next step would start with low leap onto L.

PATTERN

Measures

4   Introduction — M bows to R and L W.

            Figure I. Pas de Basque in LOD

1-8   Starting R all dance 8 Pas de Basque in LOD (CCW). On meas. 8 W move in so as to join free hands to make a circle of 3. M still facing LOD.

Figure II. Circle of Three

1-3 With hands still at shoulder height and starting with R ft., circle to L (CW) with 6 steps. On 6th step, stamp L and make ½ turn R to face CCW.

4-6 Starting R and moving CCW, walk 6 steps. On 6th step, stamp L and make ½ turn L. Take shorter steps than in meas. 1-3 so that circle does not return to starting pos.

7-9 Repeat action of meas. 1-3 (Fig. II. Take long steps so as to make certain that M passes by the spot on the circle of 3 where he is facing RLOD (of the large circle).

10-11 Starting R, walk 4 small steps to R, ending so M is facing RLOD in the large circle.

Figure III. Man Progresses to Next Circle

1-2 W raise joined hands as M drops W hands. M, with 4 steps, duck under joined hands and progress to next 2 W in circle behind. (M progresses in a CW direction in relation to the big circle.)

3 M bow to new ptrs. as W bow to new M.

4 With 2 steps M make ½ turn to R to take place between 2 W and join hands with them so all are in pos. (facing CCW) to start dance again.
Repeat above pattern to end of music. On last repetition M does not progress. Finish dance with bow to ptrs.

OBEREK OPOCZYNSKI
(O-beh-rek Opo-chenn-ski)

SOURCE: Oberek Opoczynski comes from the town of Opoczno in the central part of Poland.

MUSIC: Records — Bruno BR 50017 Side A, Band 4 "Poland in Song and Dance." 3/4 meter.
Vanguard VRS 6001 or 9016 (Song from Opoczno).

FORMATION: Cpls. in double circle facing CCW, W to R of M. Inside hands joined shoulder height, with elbows bent. M L hand free, usually extended diag. fwd. W R hand hold skirt at about finger-tip length and out a little. W does not "swish" skirt.

STEPS: *Pas de Basque:* Leap diag. fwd. on L (ct. 1). Step R in front of L (ct. 2). Step in place on L (ct. 3). *Travelling Pas de Basque:* Basically the same as pas de basque but step in LOD on ct. 2 instead of crossing. Lengthen steps so more ground can be covered.
              Turning Step: Small leap onto L with bend of knee (ct. 1). Step R (ct. 2). Step L beside R (ct. 3). Next step would start with leap onto R. Two Turning Steps are used to make 1 CW turn (as in waltz, polka, etc.).

PATTERN

Measures

4 meas.   Introduction.

Figure I

1-3   Beg. M L, W R move fwd. in LOD with 3 Pas de
             Basques.

4   Step on inside ft. (ct. 1). Tap outside ft. next to in-
             side ft. (ct. 2). Raise knee of outside ft., at same time
             lifting heel of inside ft. (ct. 3).

5-16   Repeat action of meas. 1-4 three more times (4 in all).

Figure II (Vocal)

1-6   Beg. M W, W R move ahead on 6 Travelling pas de
             basque Steps. Cover more ground than in Fig. I. On
             meas. 5-6 gradually change hand pos. to Skater's pos.
             with *L* on top.

7-8   M dance 2 Pas de Basques almost on the spot. With
             hands still joined, turn W once to L on 6 steps.

9-16   Repeat action of meas. 1-8 (Fig. II) but on meas.
             15-16 turn W to R.

17-32   Repeat action of meas. 1-16 (Fig. II). On last turn,
             M help W to place W L arm across M shoulders. M
             put R hand on W R waist. Outside hands extended
             sdwd., down and out.

Figure III (Butterfly)

1-8   With knees bent, also bend fwd. from waist. Heads
             are close together. Beg. M L, W R dance 8 pas de
             basques on the spot, turning CCW (M backing up).
             End facing ctr.

9-12   Releasing ptr., M dance 4 pas de basques in place,
             hands clasped behind back. W, hands holding skirts,
             move fwd. twd. ctr. on 4 pas de basques.

13-16   On 2 pas de basques M dance twd. ptr. At same
          time, W turn ½ CCW to face ptr. On meas. 15-16
          all join R hands with own ptr. and L with corner.
          Because hands are joined, this is one circle but actu-
          ally there is an inner circle of W facing out and an
          outer circle of M facing in.

          Figure IV

1-4   Beg. L, M dance 4 pas de basques in place. W, beg.
          R, dance 4 pas de basques turning R once around
          under joined R hands.

5-8   Repeat action of meas. 1-4 (Fig. IV) but W turn L
          once around under joined hands.

9-16   Repeat action of meas. 1-8 (Fig. IV) but M turn L
          under joined L hands and back to R while W dance
          in place.

          Figure V (Vocal)

1-4   Beg. M L, W R dance 4 pas de basques. On meas. 1
          and 2, drop joined L hands and widen circle by M
          leading W out of ctr. On meas. 3 and 4 M place W
          R hand on M L shoulder. M put own R hand on W
          R waist. R hips are adj. W hold skirt with L. M L
          hand out to side and down. Cpls. move in ½ circle
          to L so M back is to ctr.

5-16   Beg. M L, W R dance 12 Turning Steps, turning
          CW and progressing CCW in circle.
          Note: When using Vanguard record, dance ends
          here. If using Bruno record, dance Turning Step
          for 8 more meas. and then dance off the floor as the
          music fades.

OBEREK ZVICAINY — Simple

SOURCE: Learned in Poland and arranged for this record
          by Anatol Joukowsky.

MUSIC: Record — Harmonia 1015A "Oberek."

FORMATION: Circle of cpls. facing CCW, inside hands joined at waist level, M L hand in fist on his L hip. W takes skirt 8 or 10 inches below the waist (in R) and holds it up (waist level) on front of R hip (palm out, fingers bwd.). This is the skirt hold whenever R is free. Steps are indicated for M; W steps are counterpart unless otherwise indicated.

STEPS: *Pas de Basque, Walking Step, Waltz Balance.*
Mazur Step: An accented running step to 3/4 time. Accent the first beat, bringing the opposite foot up sharply in back with a knee bend. On ct. 2 the step is small and unaccented and a heavy accent on ct. 3.
Step-Close with Heel Clicks: Step to own R on R (ct. 1), close L to R (ct. 2), jump on L ft., clicking heels together in air (ct. 3).
Dish-Rag Turn: Ptrs. facing, both hands joined straight across; retaining both hand holds, M turns L under his L arm while W turns R under her R arm, to end facing ptr. in original position. Variation: W only turns once completely to R (or L), while M assists her in her turn as he dances in place.

PATTERN

Measures

1-4   Introduction: Face ptr. and bow.

1-8   *Figure I. Pas de Basque, Step-Stamp, Dish-Rag Turn*
Starting outside ft. (M L, W R), cpl. progresses fwd. in LOD with 8 pas de basque steps (in a reaching manner), turning out on outside ft., and in twd. ptr. on inside ft., swinging joined hands fwd. and bwd. (1 pas de basque step to each meas.).

9   Cpl. facing (M back to center of circle), join both hands straight across. M step L (ct. 1), bring R to L with small stamp (ct. 2), hold (ct. 3).

10   Repeat meas. 9 starting M R.

11-12 Cpl. does dish-rag turn moving CCW in Scuff as follows: Step twd. LOD (M L, W R), scuff heel (M R, W L) twd. LOD and complete turn pivoting on M L, W R. Momentum of the scuff carries you through on the pivot.

13-16 Repeat action of meas. 9-12, moving CW (starting M R, W L).

1-8   Repeat action of meas. 1-8.
(repeat)

Figure II. Pivot-Turn (Oberek Step)

1   Cpl. in semi-open pos., except M L hand is extended outward at shoulder level, and W R hand holds her skirt. M steps L with heavily accented dip, pivoting to R turning CW (cts. 1, 2, 3); W takes 3 small steps R, L, R while turning to her R.

2   M takes 3 small steps R, L, R to recover from dip of meas. 1, while W pivots R on heavy dip on L ft. (cts. 1, 2, 3).

3-16   Repeat meas. 1-2 for 7 more times (8 in all). End facing CCW. Change pos. on last meas. to starting pos., inside hands joined.
       Note: During the M dip on his L ft., he may insert heel-clicks if he prefers, as follows: Dip on L (ct. 1), click R heel against L twice (cts. 2, 3) in air. This variation is done only by the M.

1-8   Repeat action of Fig. 1, meas. 1-8.
(repeat)

Figure III. Walk with Dish-Rag Turn

1-4   Cpl. facing CCW, inside shoulders together, W L
       arm in back of M joined in his L hand over, or
       slightly above his shoulder; M R arm extended
       across in front of W, chest high, holding W R hand.
       Cpl. moves fwd. with 3 reaching pas de basque steps,
       both starting R, and reverses direction with 4th pas
       de basque. Reversal of direction is performed by
       turning in twd. ptr. without breaking hand hold.
       Cpl. now faces CW, M L hand in back of W, joined
       with her L hand over her L shoulder.

5-8   Moving bwd. cpl. repeats meas. 1-4, turning inward
       on 8th meas. to face CCW once more. During meas.
       8, both take 2 steps only, L R (cts. 1, 2) holding ct.
       3, leaving L ft. free to start next fig. M places R
       hand behind W at her waist, W holds skirt with R.

9-16   Cpl. makes 2 turns almost in place CCW (both mov-
       ing fwd. in very small circle) with following step:
       M step L (ct. 1), tap R heel beside L (ct. 2), step R
       (ct. 3). W step L (ct. 1), brush ball of R ft. slightly
       fwd. beside L (ct. 2), step R (ct. 3). Repeat step 7
       times, making 8 in all. During meas. 16 both take 3
       steps (L, R, L) ending with weight on L ft.

1-8   Repeat action of Fig. III, meas. 1-8, both completing
       8 pas de basque steps.

Figure IV. Circle Turn (Butterfly)

1-7   Cpl. in open pos. bend deeply at waist (heads of ptrs.
       adjacent, nearly touching). Outside arms are ex-
       tended sdwd. at shoulder level. Starting outside ft.
       cpl. turns twice in small circle CW, M moving fwd.,
       W bwd. using 7 small pas de basque steps.

8   M changes W to his L side by taking 3 quick steps

(R, L, R) moving slightly to his R. W makes a complete L turn in 3 steps (L, R, L) changing to M L side.

9-16   In new pos., cpl. makes two turns CCW (M again moving fwd.) with 8 small pas de basque steps, starting inside ft.

Interlude

1-4   W spins to her L away from ptr., to join hands in center and form a circle with all other W, facing out; M form circle facing in, fists on hips.

Figure V. Heel Click Step

1-3   Both circles move to R using step-close with heel click steps. Repeat step 2 more times (3 in all).

4   Take 3 stamps in place (R, L, R).

5-7   Repeat meas. 1-3 moving to L, starting L ft.

8   M takes 2 stamps (cts. 1, 2) hold ct. 3, wt. on R ft. W takes 3 stamps, L, R, L (cts. 1, 2, 3), wt. on L ft.

9-11   Facing ptr., hands joined in cross-hold pos., take 3 mazur steps (beginning M L, W R) moving out of center (M bwd., W fwd.).

12   W turn to R once without breaking hand hold (dish-rag) using 1 mazur step (L, R, L) while M does 1 mazur step in place (R, L, R).

13-16   Repeat meas. 9-12, returning to center (W bwd., M fwd.), with W turning L on 16th meas. while M takes 2 stamps (R, L) cts. 1, 2, holding ct. 3, wt. on L.

1-8
(repeat)   Repeat action of Fig. V, meas. 1-8.

9-12   Repeat action of Fig. V, meas. 9-11. On meas. 12 change to Back Hold Pos. (no dish-rag turn for W).

13-20   Cpl. turn CW (twice) in own circle with 8 mazur
         steps, M starting L, W R. End in cross-hold pos.

21-24   Beginning M L, W R (M fwd., W bwd.), return to
         center with (R, L) ending with wt. on L.

1-8   Repeat action of Fig. V, meas. 1-8, both starting R
         and moving R.

(repeat)
9-16   Moving out of center in cross-hold pos., repeat action
         of Fig. V, meas. 9-12 two times (8 mazur steps) omit-
         ting the dish-rag turns for W.
         Note: On last 3 meas. M maneuvers W (CW) to out-
         side of circle.

         Figure VI. Pivot-Turn (Oberek)
1-16   Repeat action of Fig. II, meas. 1-16 only. Join inside
         hands on meas. 16.

         Figure VII. Mazur Heel-Click and Turn
1-2   Cpl. facing, inside hands joined, free hand in fist on
         hip. Beginning M L, W R, dance 2 mazur steps
         (slightly back to back and face to face).

3-4   Moving in LOD, M starts L and does 2 heel-click
         steps, with L fist on his hip and his arm swinging
         down and up in a circle flicking W skirts (as W
         turns alone). W with fists on hips, takes 2 turns to
         her R with Scuff steps (same step as in Fig. I, meas.
         11-12).

5-6   Cpl. facing, inside hands joined, dance 1 mazur step
         to M L (LOD) and 1 mazur step to M R (RLOD).

7-8   With both hands joined straight across, cpl. does a
         dish-rag turn to M L (LOD), using scuff step. Cpl.
         bends low and close to each other on the turn.

9-32   Repeat action of Fig. VII, meas. 1-8 three more
         times (4 in all).

Figure VIII. Pas de Basque and Pose

1-6   Repeat action of Fig. I, meas. 1-6.

7-8   Ending pose: M drops to R knee, with L knee up
           and fwd. in LOD. W turns under their joined
           hands (CW) with 3 steps (L, R, L) and sits on M L
           knee, L hand in lap, R hand holding skirt at side,
           facing out of center. M R arm extended out from
           shoulder, L arm at W back.

KRAKOWIACZEK
(Krah koh ve ah′ check)

SOURCE: This is a simplified version of the Krakowiaczek
                (from the Krakow region). It was learned in Po-
                land and arranged for this record by Anatol Jou-
                kowsky.

MUSIC: Record — Mazowsze Song & Dance Ensemble of
                Poland — Bruno 50071 Side B, Band 7. 2/4 meter.

FORMATION: Cpls. in double circle, M on inside, ptrs. facing,
                inside hands (M R, W L) joined at shoulder
                height. W R hand on hip, fingers fwd. M L hand
                just behind hip, palm out. Whenever one or both
                hands are free, use these pos.

STEPS: *Pas de Basque, Sliding Step.*
                Walk: Take 2 steps to a meas. unless otherwise
                directed.
                Click Step: Hop on R, clicking heels (ct. 1). Step
                on L (ct. &). Step on R (ct. 2). Repeat of step starts
                again with hop on R. Step can start with hop on
                L and each repeat would start with hop on L.
                Balance Step: Small step swd. on R (ct. 1). Step L
                next to R (ct. &). Step R in place (ct. 2). Hold (ct.
                &). Next step would start with small step to L on
                L.

Turning Step: Small leap onto L, with bend of knee (ct. 1). Step R (ct. &). Step L next to R (ct. 2). Hold (ct. &). Next step would start with leap onto R. Two Turning Steps are used to make 1 CW turn (as in a waltz, polka, etc.).

PATTERN

Measures

1-8   Introduction.

Figure I. Back to Back, Face to Face

1-2   Beg. with M L, W R walk 3 steps in LOD (1 step to a ct.). End in back to back pos. with ptr. Touch inside ft. (M R, W L) fwd. in LOD (meas. 2, ct. 2).

3-4   Repeat 3 walking steps beg. with inside ft. and moving in LOD. End facing ptr. Touch outside ft. (M L, W R) in LOD.

5-6   In place dance 2 pas de basque steps beg. on M L, W R.

7   With 2 walking steps drop hands and change places with ptr. W pass to LOD side (pass L shoulders).

8   M: Stepping on L, make 1/2 turn to L to face ptr. (ct. 1). Close R to L (ct. 2).
W: Stepping on R, make 1/2 turn to R to face ptr. (ct. 1). Close L to R (no wt.) (ct. 2). Ptrs. should be near each other.

9-11   Join hands straight across. Put R hips adj., extending R arm in front of ptr. L elbow is bent and arms are parallel to floor. Beg. with hop on R, dance 3 Click Steps, moving in CW circle 1/2 turn to end M on inside and W on outside of circle (original places).

12   Stepping L, R in place, assume beg. pos. (meas. 1). W put no wt. on step on R.

13-96   Repeat action of meas. 1-12 (Fig. I) 7 more times (8 in all).

Note: No need to ct. how many times pattern is done. First time is danced to instruments only. Second through seventh time is danced to vocal. Last time is again to just instruments.

Figure II. Men in Center

1-4   *Men:* Beg. L ft. and making ½ turn R, walk 8 steps twd. ctr. to join hands in circle.

5   Hopping on R, click heels (ct. 1). Step L to L side (ct. 2).

6   Step R across in front of L (ct. 1). Hopping on R, click heels (ct. 2). Circle moves to L (CW) during action of meas. 5-6 (Fig. II).

7-12   Repeat action of meas. 5-6 (Fig. II) 3 more times. *Note:* Repeating the action puts 2 clicks together.

13-14   Repeat action of meas. 5-6 (Fig. II) 1 more time but drop hands and make ½ turn to L to face W. Omit last hop and click on R (meas. 14, ct. 2). Instead close L to R (no wt.).

Women: meas. 1-2: Beg. R and facing a little L of LOD, walk 3 steps in LOD. Facing ctr., close L to R (no wt.) (meas. 2, ct. 2). Hold skirts throughout this figure.

Meas. 3-4: Turning to face R LOD, walk 3 steps L, R, L. Light stamp on R next to L (no wt.) (meas. 4, ct. 2).

Meas. 5-6: Continue walk in R LOD but start R. Adjust length of step so as to keep behind ptr.

Meas. 7-10: Repeat action of meas. 3-6 (Fig. II).

Meas. 11-12: Repeat action of meas. 3-4 (Fig. II).

Meas. 13-14: Beg. R move to M on 4 walks. On last ct. of meas. 14 ptrs. take ballroom pos., M back to ctr.

Figure III. Slides in CW Circle

1-13   Beg. M L, W R take 26 Sliding Steps (2 to a meas.).
Each cpl. make ½ of a CW circle and then travel in
R LOD. M face ctr.   *Ctr.*
See diag.

R LOD

Figure IV. Women in Center

1-2   *Men:* Hands on hips and face R LOD. Walk L, R,
L. Close R to L with a click (no wt.).

3-4   Repeat action of meas. 1-2 (Fig. IV), but beg. with
R ft.

5-8   Repeat action of meas. 1-4 (Fig. IV).

9   Turning R to face ctr., step L (ct. 1). Close R to L
(no wt.) (ct. 2). Adjust length of step so as to end
facing ptr.
Women: Meas. 1: Making ½ turn R to face ctr.,
step R (ct. 1). Close L to R (no wt.) (ct. 2).
Meas. 2-9: Beg. with hop on R, dance 8 Click Steps
moving to L. If not close enough to neighbors to
join hands, move diag. in to L on Click Steps so hands
may be joined as soon as possible. Hold skirt until
hands are joined. On last Click Step drop hands and
make ½ turn R to face ptr.

Figure V. Man Lifts Woman

1-5   Beg. M R, W L dance 5 Balance Steps. On first two
move twd. ptr. On 3rd and 4th join hands straight
across. On 5th Balance Step change to shoulder-waist
pos.

6   On ct. 1 M prepare to lift W. On ct. 2 M lift W up
and to M R.

7   M put W down on outside of circle. M now has back to ctr.

8   In preparation for turn, W put R hand on M L shoulder. W L hand hold skirt. M put R hand at W waist, M L arm out to side, just below shoulder height, palm down.

Figure VI. Turn with Partner

1-13   Beg. M L, W R dance 13 Turning Steps to make 6½ CW turns moving in LOD. M end on outside of circle.

Figure VII. Finale

1-2   *Men:* Passing to R LOD side of W, walk 4 steps twd. ctr. beg. R.

3-4   On meas. 3, ct. 1 stamp R ft. and clap hands. On remaining 3 cts. bring arms fwd., up, and over to rest on neighbor's shoulders.

5   Hop on L twice (cts. 1, 2).

6   Leap to R side on R bending L knee so L leg crosses behind R knee (ct. 1). L knee is turned out to L. L ankle is just about behind R knee. Step L across behind R (ct. 2).

7-22   Repeat action of meas. 5-6 (Fig. VII) 8 more times (9 in all).

23-24   With 3 steps (R, L, R) turn R to face ptr. With hands just behind waist, stamp L.
         Women: Meas. 1-2: With 3 steps (L, R, L) make ½ turn R to face ctr. Close R to L (no wt.) (meas. 2, ct. 2). Hands on hips.
         Meas. 3-4: Beg. R and facing a little L of LOD, walk 3 steps in LOD. Facing ctr., close L to R (no wt.) (meas. 4, ct. 2).
         Meas. 5-6: Turning to face a little R of R LOD,

walk 3 steps beg. L. Facing ctr., close R to L (no wt.) (meas. 6, ct. 2).

Meas. 7-18: Repeat W action of meas. 3-6 (Fig. VII) three times.

Meas. 19-20: Repeat W action of meas. 3-4 (Fig. VII).

Meas. 21: Stamp L (no wt.) and clap hands (ct. 1). Hold (ct. 2).

Meas. 22-23: Repeat W action of meas. 21 (Fig. VII) twice (3 stamps in all). Put wt. on last stamp.

Meas. 24: Step to R side on R (ct. 1). Step L behind R and curtsey to ptr. (ct. 2).

Note: Because M circle moves CCW and W stays more or less in place, M may not end in front of ptr. In such case, W circle curtsies to M circle which finishes with stamp of L ft.

CHAPTER EIGHT

RUSSIA

Under the significant sign of USSR (Union of Soviet Socialist Republics) which contains 16 different republics, one can find many varied ethnic groups. This has come about through a long historical development of vast differences in background due to geographical, economic and religious factors.

Throughout the history of Russia interest in dance and music has been apparent. When one speaks about "Russian dance" he is referring to the dances of Velikarussia or Great Russia, a geographical location in Central Russia.

All Russian dances basically have no fixed patterns. The setting of steps, the characteristics of one or another region or district is entirely free. The pattern is left to the inspiration and

ability of the dancers. There is a typical, preferred dance form, however. It is a circle. The steps, expression of the dance are related to the local tradition and style. The Horovodnaya Pliaska is the oldest slavic dance formation. It has literally hundreds of variations.

All exhibition groups performing around the world with tremendous success are semi or entirely professional ensembles. They exhibit choreographed dances for demonstration purposes only. The Igor Moiseyev dance ensemble, and the Beriozka state company present programs of dances as a result of highly sophisticated cultural selection.

KAK U KLUCHIKA
(Cock-u-Klu-chee-kah)
(By A Spring)

Horovodnaya Pliaska — a circle dance

SOURCE: "By a Spring" is a Russian Wedding Dance performed by women. Dance comes from Yaroslav region of central Russia.

MUSIC: Records — Folk Dances — Song Colosseum CRLPX 013 Side A, Band 10. Russian Folk Songs, Stinson SLP 1003 Vol. 4, Side A, Band 6. Music in 3/4 time.

FORMATION: Closed circle of W almost facing LOD (CCW). Join hands and hold down. Heads are bowed.

STEPS: *Basic Step:* Takes 2 cts. to complete 1 step so 3 steps are done in 2 meas. In preparation for step, bend L knee on upbeat of meas. 1 and start reaching fwd. with R ft. Step fwd. R in LOD (ct. 1). Step on ball of L next to R instep (ct. &). Step fwd. R in LOD (ct. 2). Bend R knee and extend L leg diag. fwd. R, toe close to floor (ct. &). Head and body are inclined twd. extended ft. Repeat of step starts with L on ct. 3 and also uses ct. 1 of next meas.

PATTERN

Measures

4   Introduction. No action.

1-2   Dance 3 basic steps in LOD starting R (begins with vocal).

3   While turning to face ctr., move extended L leg in small arc to L and step on it (ct. 1). This would be same as "step to L side with L" if dancer had been facing ctr. at start of movement. Step R behind L, bending knees (ct. 2). Close L to R (ct. 3). Head and upper body follows direction of movement.

4   Still facing ctr., step to R side with R (ct. 1). Step L behind R, bending knees (ct. 2). Close R to L (ct. 3). Head and upper body follows direction of movements. On upbeat, bend R knee and start reaching with L to move in RLOD.

5-8   Repeat action of meas. 1-4 but starting L and moving in RLOD. Face ctr. for meas. 7-8.
           Repeat action of meas. 1-8 until end of music.

NASHEY KATE
(Our Katia)

SOURCE: Our Katia is a horovodnaya pliaska or circle dance.

MUSIC: 2/4 meter. (Special recording.) Festival Folk Shop — Out Katia.

FORMATION: Closed circle, no ptrs. Hands joined and held down.

STEPS: *Russian Polka:* Step fwd. on heel of L ft. (ct. 1). Close R to L (ct. &). Step fwd. on heel of L (ct. 2). Repeat of step beg. R.

PATTERN

Measures

20 meas.	Introduction. Dance starts with the vocal.
1-2	Beg. L, dance 2 Russian Polkas to L (RLOD).
3-4	Continuing, walk 4 steps (L, R, L, R).
5-6	Repeat action of meas. 1-2.
7	Walk 2 steps (L, R) in RLOD.
8	Step L in RLOD but turn to face ctr. (ct. 1). Step R twd. ctr. (ct. 2).
9	Stamp L beside R (no wt.) (ct. 1). Step L twd. ctr. (ct. 2).
10	Stamp R beside L (no wt.) (ct. 1). Step bkwd. on R twd. orig. pos. (ct. 2).
11-12	Continuing L, R, L back up to orig. pos. Step R twd. Str. (Meas. 12, ct. 2).
13-16	Repeat action of meas. 9-12.
17	Repeat action of meas. 9.
18	Stamp R beside L (no wt.) (ct. 1). Release hands, ex-

tend arms to sides, L high and R low, palms out and elbows straight. Starting to make a 3/4 circle CW, step R (ct. 2).

19-20   Continuing the 3/4 circle CW to reform circle of orig. size, step L, R, L. Stamp R in RLOD (meas. 20, ct. 2) and rejoin hands to start dance again.

Note: Dance is written to conform to the musical structure. When dancing it, the first part seems to end on ct. 1 of meas. 8. The second part seems to start on ct. 2 of meas. 8 and end with the 3/4 CW circle having 5 steps. When cueing the dance, it might be convenient to use a dance ct. that starts again on ct. 2 of meas. 8.

Variations for Our Katia may be done at any time by any of the dancers without disturbing others.

Variation I

No change up through meas. 8, ct. 1.

Small leap on R twd. ctr. (meas. 8, ct. 2). Stamp L heel next to R (no wt.) (meas. 8, ct. &). Small leap onto L twd. ctr. (meas. 9, ct. 1).

Stamp R heel next to L (no wt.) (meas. 9, ct. &). Bigger leap onto R twd. ctr. (meas. 9, ct. 2). Step L next to R (meas. 9, ct. &).

Stamp R next to L (no wt.) (meas. 10, ct. 1).

Dance continues as in orig. from meas. 10, ct. 2 through meas. 12, ct. 1. Do variation as given above for meas. 12, ct. 2 through meas. 14, ct. 1. Use also for meas. 16, ct. 2 through meas. 18, ct. 1. In other words this is a variation to be used when moving twd. ctr. of circle.

Variation II

To be used when backing away from ctr. Dance same as orig. through meas. 10, ct. 1.

Moving back to orig. pos., step R (meas. 10, ct. 2),

step L (ct. &), step R (meas. 11, ct. 1), step L (ct. &), step R (ct. 2), step L (ct. &). Stamp R next to L (no wt.) (meas. 12, ct. 1). Actually 6 little steps and a stamp. Use also for meas. 14, ct. 2 through meas. 16, ct. 1.

"I KTO EVO ZNAIET?"
(Who Knows)

SOURCE: This Russian dance, done by men and women in a broken circle, takes its name from the title of the song to which it is danced.

MUSIC: Records — Folk Dances-Songs Colosseum CRLPX 013 Side B, Band 1. Russian Folk Songs Stinson SLP 1003 Vol. 4, Side A, Band 4. Music is in 2/4 time.

FORMATION: Broken circle of M and W. Join hands and hold down. Free hands of end dancers on hip, palm out. Face RLOD(CW).

STEPS: *Basic Step:* Step fwd. L (ct. 1). Close R to L (ct. &). Step fwd. L (ct. 2). Brush R fwd. (ct. &). All steps are taken on flat of ft. even the brush of R ft. Repeat of step starts with R. Walking steps are done with small plié or bend of knee.
Note: Although music is played in 2/4 time, twice during the dance a half meas. (1 ct. instead of 2) is played. This is duly noted and should cause no trouble. This occurs also during the Introduction.

PATTERN

Measures

9½
(19 cts.)   Introduction. No action.

Figure I

1-5   Starting L, dance 5 basic steps in RLOD.

6   Step R (ct. 1). Step L, making ½ turn to face LOD (ct. 2).

7-11   Starting R, dance 5 basic steps in LOD(CCW).

12 (1 ct.) Step L, making ¼ turn L to face ctr. (ct. 1). There is no ct. 2.

Figure II

1   Moving twd. ctr., step fwd. flat on R, bending knee (ct. 1). Close L to R. ft. flat on floor (ct. &). Repeat for cts. 2, &.

2-4   Repeat action of meas. 1 (Fig. II) three times. On last step do not put wt. on L.

5-8   Back out of circle to place on 8 walking steps (2 to a meas.) starting L.

Figure III

1-4½   Drop hands of neighbors and extend hands fwd. and
(9 cts.)   out about hip level, palms twd. ctr. Starting L, walk 9 steps in CW(R) circle. Rejoin hands at end. R ft. will be free. (This music has 4 complete meas. and a fifth with only 1 ct.). Repeat dance from Fig. I but reversing all. Fig. I will start R(LOD) with R ft. On Fig. II L ft. will lead into ctr. Walk out starting R. Circle at end will be CCW starting with R. Dance is done 2 more times (starting to L and to R). On 5th time (starting to L) music ends after Fig. II so there is no CW circle.

QUADRILLE-POLKA

SOURCE: This is a Russian dance, using 4 cpls. in a set. It is arranged by Anatol Joukowsky for this record.

MUSIC:	Record — Beryozka Dance Ensemble in Russian Dances BR 50075 Side A, Band 1. No introduction. Music in 2/4 meter.
FORMATION:	Cpls. 1 & 4 side by side, backs to music. Cpl. 4 to L of cpl. 1. Cpls. 2 & 3 stand opp., about 6 ft. away. Cpl. 2 faces cpl. 1. Cpl. 3 faces cpl. 4. Each W to R of ptr. When hands are free, W holds skirt. M hands hang naturally at sides.
STEPS:	*Walking:* One step to a ct. Knees are relaxed and flexible.

Russian Polka: A polka with the hop omitted on the upbeat so step actually resembles a two-step.

Walk-Polka Combination: Take 2 meas. Walk R (ct. 1), L (ct. 2). Beg. R, do 1 Russian Polka (meas. 2). Next combination would start L. Used only by W.

Side Balance: Step to L side with L (ct. 1). Close R to L (no wt.) (ct. 2). May be done beg. to R with R.

PATTERN

Measures

Figure I. Honors

1-4   W stand in place. M advance to W directly opp. on 6 walking steps beg. R (3 meas.). Close R to L (meas. 4, ct. 1). Bow to opp. W (ct. 2). Cpls. 1&2, 3&4 are working together.

5-8   M, beg. L, back up to place on 6 walks. On meas. 8 close ft. together (ct. 1) and bow to ptr. (ct. 2).

9-12   M stand in place. W advance to opp. M on 6 walking steps. On meas. 12 curtesy to opp. M (R ft. behind on curtsey).

13-16   W, beg. R, back up to place on 6 walks. On meas. 16 curtsey to ptr.

Figure II. Women Star Circle

1-4   W form R hand star by extending arms but do not hold hands at ctr. Using 2 Walk-Polka Comb., beg. R, circle CW ½ way around to diag. opp. M. W 1 go to M 3, W 2 to M 4, W 3 to M 1, W 4 to M 2.

5-8   Hooking L elbows with M, circle once CCW. W use 2 Walk-Polka Comb., beg. R, M walk 8 steps.

9-12   W repeat action of meas. 1-4 (Fig. II) to return to place.

13-16   Hooking L elbows with ptr., circle once CCW. W use 2 Walk-Polka Comb., beg. R. M walk 8 steps. End facing cpl. directly opp.

Figure III. Couples Honor

1-4   Join inside hands, elbows bent, with ptr. Advance to meet opp. cpl. (Cpl. 1 to 2, etc.). M use action of Fig. I, meas. 1-4. W use action of Fig. I, meas. 9-12.

5-8   Back up to place on 8 walking steps. On last 4 steps wheel ¼ turn as a cpl., to end in place facing adj. cpl. Cpl. 1 now faces cpl. 4.

Figure VII. Women Circle

1-16   Drop hand hold. M, on 8 walks beg. R, pass L shoulder with ptr. and move to original place in set. Turn R to face ctr. of set. Stand in place for rest of Fig. W, beg. R, use Walk-Polka Combination 4 times. Move to ctr. and join hands in circle, shoulder height, elbows bent. Circle R (CCW). Circle L (CW) on 4 more Walk-Polka Combination. End in front of ptr., both facing ctr. W drop hands and hold skirt.

Figure VIII. Men Visit Women

1-2   W, beg. R, turn to R on 4 steps to face out of set. M, beg. R, walk 4 steps diag. R to face W on R.

3-4   W do 2 small Side Balance steps in place beg. R. Balances may be so small as to become a sway. M dance in front of the new W. Stamp R (ct. 1). Hit L heel next to R (no wt.) (ct. &). Stamp L next to R (ct. 2). Hit R heel next to L (no wt.) (ct. &). Stamp R, L, R (meas. 4, cts. 1 &, 2). No wt. on last stamp R. Hold ct. &.

5-16   Repeat action of meas. 1-4 (Fig. VIII) 3 more times. M travel to new W on R each time. On meas. 15-16, instead of stamps to own ptr., join 2 hands across. Both walk 3 steps to L in small circle to change places. On 4th ct. assume ballroom pos. M back to ctr.

Figure IX. Couples Polka
1-16   Polka with ptr., turning CW and travelling CCW around set.

JABLOCHKO
(Little Apple)

SOURCE: Jablochko is a Russian folk dance arranged by Anatol Joukowsky to fit recorded music.

MUSIC: Record — Stinson 3410-A.

FORMATION: Partners face each other. Partners may stand in line, or circle, hands at sides. (Throughout dance, free hands are on hips, palms out, unless otherwise indicated.)

STEPS: Small sliding walking steps (sl-wa), Buzz, Pas de Basque.
Brush Step: Step R meas. 1, ct. 1), brush L heel fwd. (ct. 2), step L (meas. 2, ct. 1), step R, turning ½ CCW (ct. 2). Next step starts L, with ½ turn CW on last ct.
Brush Step Variation: Step R (meas. 1, ct. 1), brush L heel fwd. (ct. 2), step L (meas. 2, ct. 1), step R (ct. &), step L (ct. 2), hold (ct. &). Step always starts R.

Slap Step: Step R (meas. 1, ct. 1), slap L ft. on out-side of heel with L hand, L ft. brought up behind to knee level (ct. 2), step L (meas. 2, ct. 1), step R turning ½ CCW (ct. 2). Next step starts L, with ½ turn CW on last ct.

Slap Step — Variation I: Step R (meas. 1, ct. 1), slap L (ct. 2), step L (meas. 2, ct. 1), step R (ct. &), step L (ct. 2), hold (ct. &). Step always starts R.

Slap Step — Variation II: Step R (meas. 1, ct. 1), slap L (ct. 2), step L (meas. 2, ct. 1), step R (ct. &), stamp L, no wt. (ct. 2) hold (ct. &). Next step starts L, with *turn on meas. 1, ct. 1.*

Rest Step: W: Step R (ct. 1) touch L heel, toe out (no wt.), at R instep, turning body twd. L (ct. 2). Next step starts L. M: Same step, except that he stamps (lightly) on ct. 2 — more vigorous than W.

Stamping Step: Stamping step R (meas. 1, ct. 1), stamp L heel, no wt., (ct. &). Stamping step L (ct. 2), stamp R heel, no wt. (ct. &), stamping step R (meas. 2, ct. 1), stamping step L (ct. &), stamp-ing step R (ct. 2), hold (ct. &). Make ½ turn CCW on meas. 2, cts. 1&2. Next step starts L, with ½ turn CW on meas. 2, cts. 1&2.

Stamping Step Variation: Stamping step R (meas. 1, ct. 1), stamp L heel, no wt. (ct. &), stamping step L (ct. 2), stamp R heel, no wt., (ct. &), stamping step R (meas. 2, ct. 1), stamping step L (ct. &), stamp R, no wt. (ct. 2), hold (ct. &). Step always starts R.

Extending Step: Fall heavily onto L, landing with knee bent and R ft. extended fwd. slightly off floor (ct. 1&), pull wt. up in recovering with quick steps R L (cts. 2&). Start next step with fall onto R.

Russian Skip: Starting R behind L, displace each ft. alternately (remaining in place). Ct. 1 for each step.

PATTERN

Measures

Figure I. Walk and Brush

1-4   a. 4 steps fwd. Shake hands with partner.

5-8   7 walking steps once around CW in individual small circle, ending with stamp. (no wt.).

9-12   7 walking steps CCW in small individual circle, ending with stamp. (no wt.).

1-4   b. 1 brush step, M moving RLOD, W LOD.
            1 brush step, M moving LOD, W RLOD.

5-12   Repeat action of b, meas. 1-4 two more times.

Figure II. M Slap Solo

1-4   a. 1 slap step RLOD (turning ½ CCW on last ct.)
            1 slap step LOD (turning ½ CW on last ct.)

5-12   Repeat action of Fig. II, meas. 1-4 two more times.

1-12   b. M circles W once around CW with 6 Slap Step Variation I.
            During all of M solo W does Rest Step.

Figure III. W Brush Solo

1-4   a. 1 brush step, starting R and moving LOD. As ft. is brushed fwd. same hand is brought from hip and turned up at waist level, arm extended from elbow.
            1 brush step starting L and moving RLOD. Same hand movement as above.

5-12   Repeat action of Fig. III, meas. 1-4, two more times.

1-8   b. W circle M once around CW with 4 brush step variations. As ft. is brushed fwd., L hand is brought from hip and turned palm up at waist level, arm extended from elbow.

9-12   8 walking steps turning once CW in a very small
            circle.
            Throughout W solo, M does Rest Step.

Figure IV. M Stamp Solo

1-12   a. M circle W once around CW with 6 stamping
                step variations, always starting R.

1-4   b. 1 stamping step starting R and moving RLOD.
                1 stamping step starting L and moving LOD.

5-8   Repeat action of Fig. IV, b, meas. 1-4.

9-12   6 walking steps turning once CW in a small cir-
            cle, ending with a stamp R (meas. 12, ct. 1), pose
            with L heel fwd. on floor, L arm extended low in
            front, R hand high (ct. 2).
            Throughout M solo W does Rest Step.

Figure V. W Extending Step Solo

1-12   a. 4 extending steps in place.
                8 extending steps turning once CW in small cir-
                cle.

1-8   b. 8 extending steps circling M once around CW.
                7 buzz steps turning CW in place. On last ct. as-
                sume open position with partner, M L arm ex-
                tended at waist level.
                Throughout W solo, M does Rest Step until last
                meas. when he approaches W with 4 steps to as-
                sume open position for next step.

Figure VI. Pas de Basque, Brush, Solo and Buzz

1-12   a. Beginning R, 8 pas de basques LOD.
                4 pas de basques turning CCW with partner in
                small circle.

1-12   Repeat action of Fig. VI, a, meas. 1-12.
(repeated)

1-12   b. Repeat action of Fig. I, b, meas. 1-12.

1-12   c. M repeats action of Fig. II, a, meas. 1-12 using
(repeated)   Variation II. W dances small buzz steps in place,
                  turning CW twice around.

Figure VII. Walking Turn

1-12   Ptrs. advance twd. each other with 4 gliding walking
               steps, starting R. Bring hands from hips, fwd. and
               out until arms are outstretched with L higher than
               R. With 4 steps move bwd. to pos., returning hands
               to hips. Ptrs. again move twd. each other and turn
               together in a small circle CW. As ptrs. move fwd.,
               outstretch arms as before and keep outstretched dur-
               ing turn. Finish in own pos. with hands on hips.

Figure VIII. Russian Skip, Buzz and Pose

1-6   Beginning R. M and W dance 12 Russian Skip steps
               in place.

7-12   Advance twd. partner with 4 sl-wa steps and with R
               on partner's waist (L high) buzz in place. On last ct.
               (backs to center) stamp and pose, W on M R arm
               and outside arms (M L, W R) high.

V LESU PRIFRONTOVOM
(In The Forest)

SOURCE: Russian folk-waltz arranged to record by Anatol
               Joukowsky.

MUSIC: Records — Stinson 3130-A V Lesu Prifrontovom.
               Colosseum 144A Folk Dances and Songs from
               Russia (LP) Band 3: In the Forest.

FORMATION: Double circle, M on inside, ptrs. facing. Unless
               otherwise stated, W holds skirts, M has L hand
               on hip, R hand at side.

STEPS: Waltz, Waltz Balance, Pivot. Directions same for
               M and W unless otherwise stated. 3/4 time.

PATTERN

Measures

Introduction.

4   M: Step R (meas. 1). Close L to R (meas. 2). Step L (meas. 3). Close R to L with bow from waist (meas. 4). Hands at sides.

W: Step R (meas. 1). Step L behind R and bend L knee in curtsey (meas. 2). Rise and return wt. to R (meas. 3). Step L and close R to L (meas. 4). Hands on skirts.

Figure I. Waltz and Cross Over

A 1-4   Starting with R, do 4 waltz steps. On first step make ¼ turn to R. M circle CW, W CCW. Pass ptr. and next person. On 4th waltz face 3rd person in opp. circle (count ptr. as no. 1).

5-8   Join R hands. Waltz balance to new ptr. (3rd person) on R (meas. 5). Waltz balance back on L (meas. 5). Waltz balance back on L (meas. 6). Step fwd. R and pivot ½ turn L so couples change places, hands still joined (meas. 7). Step back on L and close R to L, no wt. (meas. 8).

9-12   Repeat meas. 1-4 returning to original ptr. Because of changing places, M circle CCW, W CW.

13-16   Repeat meas. 5-8 changing places with original ptr.

17-24   Repeat meas. 1-8 again changing places with new ptr. (3rd person).

25-32   In ballroom pos., waltz 8 meas. turning CW and progressing in LOD M start R, W L. M start and end in outer circle.

1-8 (rptd)   Repeat meas. 1-8 changing places with original ptr. M circle CCW, W CW.

9-16   Repeat meas. 1-8 changing places with new ptr. (3rd person). M circle CW, W CCW.

17-24   Repeat meas. 1-8 changing places with original ptr. M circle CCW, W CW.

25-32   In ballroom pos., waltz 8 meas. turning CW and progressing in LOD. M start L, W R. 4 complete turns should be made.

Figure II. Ballroom Waltz and Women Progress

B 1-6   Still in ballroom pos. continue waltz in LOD making 3 more complete turns.

7-8   Waltzing in place M turn W under joined hands fwd. to next M. W make 1 turn on 2 waltzes.

9-16   With new ptr. (2nd person) repeat meas. 1-8. Turn W on to next M.

17-24   With new ptr. (3rd person) repeat meas. 1-8. Turn W on to next M. (ptr. 4).

25-28   With just a glance at ptr. 4, waltz back to original ptr. Start with L ft. M circle CCW, W CW.

29-32   With original ptr., repeat Introduction. Start L instead of R.

Figure III. Waltz and Cross Over

A 1-32   Repeat Fig. I, meas. 1-32 only.
         Note: This will leave cpls. with new ptr. (3rd person). M in outer circle.

Figure IV. Circle and Basket

1-8 (rptd) All start R ft. M: join hands in outer circle and travel LOD 7 waltz steps. Count 7 W after last ptr. On 8th meas. waltz fwd. and bring hands over W heads to make basket. M is between W 7 and W 8. W: on first waltz turn R to face center of circle, join hands and circle CW.

9-16   Circle in basket CW (direction W were going).

17-24   Reverse direction and circle CCW. On meas. 23 and 24 raise arms to undo basket.

| 25-28 | Hands still joined M waltz CW. On first waltz, W release hands, make ½ turn R and rejoin hands. W circle CCW. Stop facing *Original ptr.* |
| 29-32 | With original ptr. join R hands and do Cross Over pattern (Fig. I, meas. 5-8). |

Figure V. Ballroom Waltz and Women Progress

| B 1-28 | Repeat Fig. II meas. 1-28. |
| 29-32 | Assume ballroom pos. with original ptr. Pause in music takes place of meas. 21-32. |

Figure VI. Waltz and Bow

Coda 1-6	Waltz in LOD (turning CW) 3 complete turns.
7	M turn W under joined hands. W step R and pivot R to face ptr.
8 and chord	Join R hands. M bow from waist, ft. together. W step L and cross R behind to make curtsey.

ORLOVSKAYA
(Or Lov skah' ya)
(Dance from Orel)

SOURCE:	Orlovskaya is a couple dance from the region of Orel in central Russia.
MUSIC:	Records — Moiseyev Dance Ensemble — Bruno BR 50046 Side A, Band 1 Polyanka. Moiseyev Russian Folk Ballet Co. — Epic LC 3459 Side 1, Band 5 Polianka. 4/4 and 2/4 time.
FORMATION:	6-10 cpls. in a set as for a contra dance. Line of M facing line of W with ptrs. opp. each other. M L shoulders twd. music (head of hall). Hands on hips, palms out.
STEPS:	Walking steps are done with small plié or bend of knee. Unless otherwise given, free hands are on hips, palm out.

Travelling Step: (1 to 2 meas.) Run L (ct. L) R (ct. 2). Still running, step flat on L bending the L knee while lifting bent R knee (meas. 2, ct. 1). Still running, step on ball of R (ct. 2). Step always starts on L.

PATTERN

Measures

4/4 time   Introduction — *The Bows*

1-8   Turn ¼ to own R and bow. L hand on hip. With R hand make sweeping gesture up, out and down (meas. 1-2). Turn ½ to L and bow. R hand on hip and L makes sweeping gesture (meas. 3-4). Make ¼ turn R to face ptr. and bow with both hands coming from hips to make sweeping gesture (meas. 5-6). Return hands to hips, palms out and stand facing ptr. (meas. 7-8).

Figure I. Slow Walk

9-10   Walk to own R, stepping R, L, R, 2 steps to a meas. Turning L to look at ptr., stamp L (no wt.).

11-12   Repeat action of meas. 9-10 but start to L with L.

13-14   Walk twd. ptr. 3 steps (R, L, R) to end back to back, R shldrs. adjacent. Stamp L (no wt.).

15-16   Back up to place, walking L, R, L. Facing ptr., close R to L (no wt.).

2/4 time   *Figure II. Balance to Ptr. and Circle*

1-2   Step twd. ptr. on R, turning R shoulder to ptr. (meas. 1). Close L to R (no wt.) (meas. 2).

3-4   Step back to place on L (meas. 3). Close R to L (no wt.) (meas. 4).

5-8   Repeat action of meas. 1-4 (Fig. II).

9-15   With 7 steps (1 to a meas.), starting R, walk in CW circle with ptr., keeping R shoulder pointed twd. ptr. End facing ptr.

16   Close L to R (no wt.).

17-24   Repeat action of meas. 1-8 (Fig. II) but start with L.

25-31   With 7 steps (1 to a meas.), starting L, walk in CCW circle with ptr., keeping L shldr. pointed twd. ptr.

32   Do 3 fast stamps (R, L, R) to finish facing ptr. W put no wt. on last stamp on R.

Figure III. Woman Circles Man

1-8   M: Hands on hips, stamp L on ct. 1 of meas. 1, 3, 5, 7.
        W: With 16 small steps (2 to a meas.) starting R, make CW circle around M. End ptrs. facing.

9-10   M: Step on L (ct. 1). Stamp R heel near L instep, toe turned out (no wt.) (ct. 2). Repeat starting R for meas. 10.
        W: Small step to R on R, moving R shoulder slightly twd. ptr. (ct. 1). Close to R (no wt.) (ct. 2). Repeat starting L for meas. 10.

11-14   Both: Repeat action of meas. 9-10 (Fig. III) two more times.

15   Both: Repeat action of meas. 9 (Fig. III).

16   M: Do 3 fast stamps R, L, R (cts. 1, & 2).
        W: Repeat action of meas. 10 (Fig. III).

Figure IV. Taking Turns

1-3   M stamp L on ct. 1 of each meas. W watch M.

4   M finish with 3 fast stamps L, R, L (ct. 1, & 2). W still watch M.

5-8   W, moving to R and away from M, make 1 CW circle on 8 small steps starting R (2 steps to a meas.). M watch W.

9-12   Repeat action of meas. 1-4 (Fig. IV) but with M stamping R.

13-16   Repeat action of meas. 5-8 (Fig. IV) but with W moving to L and away from M to make 1 CCW circle. W start with L (no wt. on last step on R).

Figure V. Arches

1-8   M join hands in a line. W hands on hips. Starting R, the 2 lines walk twds. each other. W duck under arches passing ptr. by R sides. After ducking and arching, lines move to ptr. pos. All turn R to face ptr., M dropping hands. Take 16 small steps, 2 to a meas., for the figure.

9-16   Repeat action of meas. 1-8 (Fig. V) but with W arching. Still pass R sides. End in original place facing ptr.

Figure VI. Man Prysladkas

1-16   M: Do 8 heel prysiadkas (squat-meas. 1; land on heels — meas. 2). Use arms naturally as needed for balance.
          W. Meas. L: Step to R on R. Meas. 2: Step L behind R, bending knees with L shoulder following L ft. W now almost faces foot of set. Meas. 3: Step R, turning R to face diag. L of the head of set with L shoulder pointing diag. twd. ptr. (ct. 1). Step L next to R (ct. 2). Meas. 4: Step R in place (ct. 1). Hold (ct. 2). Meas. 5-8: Repeat action of meas. 1-4 Fig. VI, but starting with L. First step on L will be diag. bkwds. twd. beginning pos. On stepping R behind L, almost face head of set. Do the 3 quick steps facing diag. R of ft. of set with R shoulder pointing diag. twd. ptr. Meas. 9-16: Repeat action of meas. 1-8 (Fig. VI). During all of Fig. keep eyes on ptr.

Figure VII. Couple Turn

1-14   Starting R, meet ptr. and turn CW with 28 small walking steps (2 to a meas.). Turn pos: Hook R arms as if for an elbow turn but instead straighten R elbow and hold stiff. Place R hand at ctr. of ptr. back. Hold L arm low and out to side. At end of turn M should face head of set and W ft. of set.

15-16 M dance 4 steps in place as W makes ½ turn to R to end facing head of set (no wt. on last step for W). W hooks L arm in M bent R arm. Cpls. now in dine all facing head of hall.

Figure VIII. Set Moves Forward and Back to Place
1 Stamp inside ft. (M R, W L), toe turned out and bending knee, at heel of outside ft. (ct. 1). Step fwd. on outside ft. (toe pointing in LOD) (ct. 2).

2-8 Repeat action of meas. 1 (Fig. VIII) 7 more times. Finish with wt. on M L, W R.

9 Moving bkwd., M step on ball of R ft. (W L) (ct. 1). M step bkwd. on ball of L ft. (W R) (ct. 2). Drop onto flat of ft. (M R, W L), extending other ft. fwd. with toe turned out (ct. 2). Body turns slightly in direction of pointing toe. While dancing, slide arms from hooked pos. to inside hands joined.

10 Repeat action of meas. 9 (Fig. VIII) but start with M L, W R.

11-14 Repeat action of meas. 9-10 (Fig. VIII) 2 more times.

15 Repeat action of meas. 9 (Fig. VIII).

16 M stamp L, R (cts. 1, 2). W stamp R, L. End facing ptr.

Figure IX. Dishrag Turns
1 With inside hands still joined, step to side on M L, W R and make full pivot turn to M L, W R to end facing ptr.

2 Dance 3 steps in place facing ptr. (cts. 1, &, 2). M start R, W L.

3-8	Repeat action of meas. 1-2 three more times. End facing ptr.
9	Both stamp R, once, M clap and W hands on hips.
10	M stamp L. Knees are slightly bent and arms are ready to help with following turn. W stamp R again.
11-12	M: Pivot to R on R once around (meas. 11). L close to floor. Stop turn by stepping on L (meas. 12). Use arms naturally to help in turn. W: Turn to R once around in 4 steps (2 to a meas.) starting with R, hands on hips.
13-16	Repeat action of meas. 9-12 (Fig. IX).

Figure X. The Bridge

1-32   Form a bridge by joining M R and W L hands and facing the head of the hall. First cpl. turns in and travels down under the bridge. As soon as they are started the second cpl. follows and so on. Cpls. forming the bridge move up as the ones ahead duck down under the bridge. When end of bridge is reached, M turns to his R (W L), joins inside hands with ptr. and moves up the set in bridge formation. All cpls. back in original pos. by end of music. When part of bridge with inside hands joined, use same step as in (Fig. VIII), meas. 1-8. When going under the bridge use small walking steps (2 to a meas.). Pos. for going under bridge: Join R hands at M back. M put L hand on W L shoulder. W put L hand on hip. Crouch down with heads together. Cpls. finish facing head of hall with inside hands joined.

Figure XI. Forming a Circle

1-16   First M lead set into CW circle using 8 Traveling Steps.

Each W joins R hand with L of M behind.

As soon as possible 1st M and last W join hands to complete circle.

Figure XII. Prysiadkas in the Circle

1-6   Drop hands. Facing ctr. of circle, M do 3 heel pry-
       siadkas (1 to 2 meas.). W repeat action of Fig. VI.
       (This takes 16 meas. so no further directions are
       given for W).

7-8   Starting R, M walk 4 steps into circle and turn to
       face ptr., back to ctr.

9-16   M do 4 heel prysiadkas (1 to 2 meas.).

Figure XIII. Finale

1-4   With R arm around ptr. R hips adjacent, turn CW
       with ptr. with 8 quick walking steps (2 to a meas.).
       Start R ft. and hold L arm high.

5-8   Continuing cpl. turn, dance 4 buzz steps (Flat on
       R-ct. 1; Up on ball of L-ct. 2).

9-12   Repeat action of meas. 1-4 (Fig. XIII).

13-14 Dance 2 buzz steps. End with W on outside of circle.

15-16 With lead from M, W turns to R 1 ½ times on 4
       steps. End facing LOD with inside hands joined and
       outside hands raised. M may accent ending with a
       stamp.

CHAPTER NINE

THE UKRAINE

The Ukraine is located at the southern part of the Soviet Union between great Russia and the Black Sea. Roughly 40 million people live in this area. Ukraine means borderland from Russian land. The Cossack is the permanent warrior here, and the life of the people is a constant struggle day and night. The Cossack may be at home one day then not home again for a whole year. The songs and dances from the Ukraine are famous all over Russia and are now spreading out from this land. The author's father was born in the Ukraine and so was the author, but the latter was too young when he left ever to call himself an Ukrainian.

Two dances are selected for this book, one from the Poltava region, the Eastern Ukrainian, another from the Western Ukraine Carpathian-land called the Hutzuls.

Each area has a different kind of people, different costumes, and different life. One in the plains, the other in the mountains. In Eastern Ukraine the people wear boots and wide blue sharovari-pants and embroidered shirts. Slacks and the mountain-type dress of Hutzuls are quite different. But all are brothers, with the same blood, same beliefs, same language — all Ukrainians. The first dance, a Kozachok is named "Bandura." It is usually accompanied by an old Ukrainian string instrument. Kozachok means the happy dance of Ukraine; a Hopak-type dance. The story of "Bandura" starts when the man dancer looks for the best woman and offers to buy her to dance with him. She is not for sale. She makes this clear by accepting the love without any gifts and finally she dances with him. No patterns, per se, exist, it is a free dance with same steps but in dif-

fering patterns and differing succession. It is slow moving in the beginning then gets faster and faster.

When doing this dance in class use the synchronized, harmonized version of the record. This is in a pattern, authentic Ukrainian steps with a "Ukrainian" feeling. Exhibition dance is complicated and composed of many fantastic combinations. Try to see here the happy, emancipated Ukrainian girls doing the same strong steps with the same strong expression as the man uses with one exception — the prysiadkas — which is a typical man's step never done by a girl.

The second dance is the Hutzulka from Western Ukraine. This is a circle dance. It repeats the melody all the time and the boy involves the girl in integrated combinations. Again, the dance can be arranged in any pattern, and it reflects in technique the feeling of being on the Carpathian slopes and the Hutzul hills southwest of the Ukrainian plains.

HUTZULKA
(Hoot sool' kah)

SOURCE: Hutzulka is a traditional dance from the Ukrainian slopes of the Carpathian Mountains. The people in the area are called the Hutzuls, whence
comes the name.

MUSIC: Records — Bruno BR 50046 Side A, Band 6
"Dances Made Famous by the Moiseyev Dance
Ensemble" 2/4 meter.
Bruno BR 50002 Side A, Band 1 "An Evening
with the Zaporozhsky Cossacks."
Monitor MF 301 Side 1, Band 2 (Hutsulka)
"Songs and Dances of the Ukraine."

FORMATION: Double circle. W on inside with backs to ctr.,
hands joined. M on outside facing ctr., hands
joined. Ptrs. facing.

STEPS: *Basic Step* (1 to 2 meas.): Step on R (ct. 1). Hop
on R (ct. &). Step on L (ct. 2), hop on L (ct. &).
Step R, L, R, L (meas. 2). On each hop, side of
free ft. taps calf of supporting leg. Step always
begins on R.
Woman's Solo Step I (1 to 2 meas.): Step on R
behind L (ct. 1). Hop on R, bringing L around
behind R (ct. &). Step on L behind R (ct. 2). Hop
on L, bringing R around behind L (ct. &). Step on
R behind L (meas. 2, ct. 1). Hop on R (ct. &).
Step fwd. L (ct. 2), R (ct. &) to compensate for
any bwd. movement in first part of step. Repeat
of step would start with step-hop on L.
Woman's Solo Step II (1 to 2 meas.): Facing ptr.,
pas de basque to R and L (meas. 1). Step-hop R
and L, traveling to R (meas. 2).
Pas de Basque (2 to a meas.): Step R to R side (ct.

1). Step L in front of R (ct. ah). Step R in place (ct. &). Repeat to L side beg. L (cts. 2, ah, &). Steps are small.

Man's Solo Step (1 to meas.): Step R across in front of L with an accent, bending knee (ct. 1). R shoulder follows R ft. Step on L in place, raising R leg, almost straight (ct. 2). Step R to R side (meas. 2, ct. 1). Stamp L in front of R (ct. 2). Step R in place (ct. &). Repeat of step starts with L crossing R.

Promenade Pos.: R hands joined and held at W R waist. L hands joined and extended fwd.

Travelling Pos: R hands same as for Promenade Pos. W L hand on M R shoulder. M L hand free.

PATTERN

Measures

Figure I. Double Circle

1-8 Beg. R ft., all circle to own R with 4 Basic Steps. W move CW, M CCW. On last 4 steps, prepare to reverse direction.

9-16 Repeat action of meas. 1-8 but circle to L, end facing ptr.

Figure II. Woman's Solo I

1-8 W: Hands on hips, fingers fwd. Dance 4 Solo Step I facing ptr.
M: Stand in stride pos., hands clasped behind back. Meas. 1: Shift wt. onto R with bend of R knee (ct. 1). Ball of L ft. remains on floor. Bend R knee 3 more times (cts. &, 2, &). Meas. 2: Repeat action of meas. 1 (Fig. II) but shift wt. onto L. Meas. 3-8: Repeat action of meas. 1-2 (Fig. II) 3 more times.

Figure III. Man's Solo

1-8 M: Beg. crossing R, dance 4 M Solo Steps facing ptr.

W: Meas. 1: Step R to R (ct. 1). Lightly touch toe of L behind R (ct. 2). Meas. 2: Repeat action of meas. 1 (Fig. III) but step L to L side. On cts. 1, &, 2, & of each meas. bend supporting knee so as to shake. Meas. 3-8: Repeat action of meas. 1-2 (Fig. III) 3 more times.

Figure IV. Basic Step

1-2 Beg. R, dance 1 Basic Step. W dance in place. M move fwd. and take W L hand in M R hand.

3-4 On 1 Basic Step widen the circle. M draw W away from ctr.

5-8 Take Promenade pos. Dance 2 Basic Steps, turning CCW on the spot.

9-14 Change to Travelling pos. Dance 3 Basic Steps travelling in LOD.

15-16 Dance 1 more Basic Step. On the step-hops, wheel 1/4 CCW and move in to narrow circle a little. On the 4 steps, release hands and end with double circle, W on inside (back to ctr.). M face ctr. Join R hand with ptr. and L with corner.

Figure V. Prysiadkas

1 W stand in place and give support to M. M squat, sitting over heels (ct. 1). Shift wt., sitting over R heel, and extend L ft. fwd. (ct. 2).

2 M shift wt., sitting over L heel, and extend R ft. fwd. (ct. 1). M shift wt., sitting over R heel, and extend L ft. fwd. (ct. 2).

3-7 Repeat action of meas. 2 (Fig. V) 5 more times (13 heel thrusts).

8 M put ft. together (ct. 1). Rise with a jump (ct. 2). W assist M. Formation is still double circle, W back to ctr., M facing ctr.

Figure VI. Travel in RLOD

1-8   W fold arms. Dance 4 W Solo Step II travelling in RLOD. M dance 4 Basic Steps travelling in RLOD, staying beside ptr. When hopping on R (meas. 1, ct. &) M slap top of L knee with L hand.

9-12   M take W L hand with R. Both dance 2 Basic Steps in RLOD, also widening the circle. On last 4 steps change to Pomenade pos.

13-16   Dance 2 Basic Steps turning CCW on the spot. On last 4 steps form a double circle, M on inside, ptrs. facing. M hands free. W hands on hips, fingers fwd.

Figure VII. Both Solo

1-8   M dance 4 M Solo Steps. W dance 4 W Solo Step I.

9-12   Assume Travelling pos. Dance 2 Basic Steps in LOD.

13-16   On 2 Basic Steps form single circle, turning 1/4 CCW to face ctr. M join hands behind W backs (narrow circle if necessary). W put hands on shoulders of adjacent M.

Figure VIII. Women's Wheel

1-8   W slide heels twd. ctr. to make a wheel pattern. Support comes from M shoulders and the W heels. Move wheel to L (CW) by moving heels along floor. M crouch just enough to adjust wheel. M move to L by stepping L (ct. 1). Close R to L (ct. &). Repeat for cts. 2, &. Continue to end of phrase.

9-16   M. help W up and assume Travelling pos. Pick up Basic Step as soon as possible and exit off floor.

BANDURA KOZATCHOK
(Koz'at chauk)
(Little Cossack)

SOURCE: The Bandura is a folk instrument used since the 16th century. This is an arrangement of typical

Ukrainian steps. The dance tells a story of a boy offering a gift to his girl and of her final acceptance of it.

MUSIC: Records — An Evening with the Zaporozhsky Cossacks. Bruno BR 50002, Side B, Band 1.
                Songs and Dances of the Ukraine. Vol. L, Monitor MF 301 Side 2, Band 2.

FORMATION: Double circle, ptnrs. facing, about 6 ft. apart. W on inside with back to ctr. M on outside facing ctr. W has back of hands on hips. M has hands clasped behind back. M has a gift in his pocket — a flower, a ribbon, a necklace, a pair of shoes, etc.

STEPS: *Walk, Pas de Basque.*
                Russian Skip: Timing same as ordinary skip but knees are turned out and each step is behind other gt. Done in place unless otherwise directed.
                Prysiadka (1 to 2 meas.): Assume squatting pos. with knees turn out, back erect (meas. 1). Hands may be on hips or drop between knees. Rise as indicated in description (meas. 2).
                Buzz Step: This is slower than usual. Step flat on R (ct. 1). Push off with L toe (ct. 2).
                Duck Walk: Assume squatting pos., head and trunk straight (ct. 1). Arms folded or hands on hips. Still in squat pos., bring L ft. in arc from back to front and step fwd. on L (ct. 2). Next step would be done with R and continue alternately as long as desired.

PATTERN

Measures

4/4 meter   No introduction.

Figure I. Slow Walk and Circling
1-2   Beg. R, both walk 7 slow steps (1 to a ct.) to own R.

Close L to R (meas. 2, ct. 4) (no wt.) and prepare to change direction.

3-4   Beg. L, walk 7 slow steps to own L. Close R to L (no wt.). Finish facing ptnr.

5-8   Beg. R, make 1 CW circle with ptnr. Keep R shoulders twd. ptnr. and watch ptnr. Step R, L, R, close L to R (no wt.) (meas. 5). Step L, R, L, close R to L (no wt.) (meas. 6). This will complete ½ of the circle. Repeat action of meas. 5-6 to complete the circle and finish in place, ptnrs. facing.

Figure II. Presenting the Gift

1-2   W watch as M presents the gift. M take gift from pocket with a large gesture and place it on floor in front of W.

3   M walk 4 steps (R, L, R, close L to R) to stand on L side of W.

4   M point to gift with L hand while place R arm around W shoulders.

5   W shrug off M arm and walk to own R 3 steps R, L, R and close L to R (no wt.). M folds arms and watches W.

6   Beg. L W walk back to place and close R to L (no wt.) all the while observing the gift.

7   Beg. R walk to gift with 3 steps and close L to R (no wt.). W finishes almost facing LOD.

8   W lightly kicks gift with L ft. and looks at M. Gift should be kicked in general area of where M stood at start of dance.

9-12   Beg. L, W walk 4 steps back to her original place. At same time M take 16 cts. to walk over, pick up gift, put it in pocket, and face ptnr. W just watch M after meas. 9.

13-14   Beg. R, with 8 walking steps, change places passing
        L shoulders, making a small CCW arc. Finish with
        ½ turn L to face ptnr. Both have back of hands on
        hips.

15-16   With 8 more steps, retrace arc passing R shoulders
        and return to place. W finish with ½ turn R to face
        M. M finish with full turn R to end with back to
        ptnr. (and ctr.), arms folded. M is irked with ptnr.
        Ptnrs. are about 2 ft. apart.

2/4 meter   *Figure III. Woman Teases Man*
  1-2   M stands ignoring ptnr. W still have back of hands
        on hips. W now try to attract M attention.
        W: Step R twd. M (meas. 1, ct. 1). With lift of R
        heel, nudge M with R elbow (ct. 2). Step back to
        place L, R, L (meas. 2, cts. 1 & 2).

  3-6   W repeat action of meas. 1-2 (Fig. III) 2 more times.
        M still ignore W.

  7-8   Beg. R, W walk 3 steps in CW arc to stand on out-
        side of circle trying to face M. Close L to R (no wt.)
        (meas. 8, ct. 2). M turn ½ around to L in place on
        4 steps to face ctr. and again present back to W.

  9-14 Beg. L, W repeat action of meas. 1-6 (Fig. III). M
        ignore W.

15-16   W turn L in place to finish facing LOD. Step L, R,
        L, close R to L (no wt.). M turn ¼ to R with 4 steps
        beg. R and place R arm around W waist, holding
        W R hand on her R waist. W put L hand on M R
        shoulder. M extend L arm diag. L, palm up. Cpls.
        now facing LOD.

        Figure IV. Pas de Basque
  1-8   Beg. R, dance 8 pas de basques in LOD (CCW).

  9-14 Turn in place CCW (2 or 3 times) with 6 pas de
        basques.

15-16   On 2 pas de basques, M lead W over to M L side. Hand pos. same as before but reversed.

17-23   Turn in place CW with 7 pas de basques.

24   M release W so W is on inside of double circle with back to ctr. Ptnrs. are facing.

Figure V. Skips and Prysiadkas

1-3   M watch W and clap on ct. 1 of meas. 1-4 (Fig. V). Beg. R behind L, W dance 6 Russian Skip steps backing up a little. Hands on hips. On upbeat of meas. 4, take small hop on L.

4   Moving fwd. a little, W step R, L, R, L.

5-8   Repeat action of meas. 1-4 (Fig. V). M still claps.

9-16   M do 4 prysiadkas landing on heels. Use arms naturally. W make CW circle around M with 8 pas de basques beg. R. Finish ptrs. facing with W back to ctr.

17-24   Beg. R, M make CW circle around W with 6 pas de basques (meas. 17-22). Back of hands on hips. End facing ptr. (and ctr.). On meas. 23-24 M do 1 prysiadka, landing with wt. on R ft. and L heel touching floor. Arms extended naturally.
Note: Instead M can circle W with 14 Duck Walk steps and rise up on meas. 24 to same ending pose as with the prysiadka. W turn once slowly to R with 8 slow Buzz Steps, R hand high, back of L hand on hip.

Figure VI. Woman Accepts the Gift

1-8   M: With 4 steps pass W by R shoulders and go into ctr. (meas. 1-2). Gesture to other M to meet in the ctr. and each take gift out of pocket, placing it in L hand (meas. 3-6). Return to outer circle with 4 steps beg. R and offer gift to ptr. (meas. 7-8).
W: Dance 4 pas de basques in LOD, beg. R (meas.

1-4). On first pas de basque (when passing R shoulder with M) move a little out of ctr. so as to widen circle. Begin with back of hands on hips and gradually extend them fwd. and out, palms up. Making ½ turn CW, dance 4 more pas de basques in RLOD back to ptr. (meas. 5-8). On last meas. accept gift from M with R hand.

9-24   M put R arm around W waist and extend L hand diag. out, palm up. W place L hand on M R shoulder and hold gift in R hand which is extended out diag. to R. Both beg. R, dance 14 pas de basques turning CCW, M backing up, W going fwd. On meas. 15-16 M start as if to change W to L side as in Fig. IV, meas. 15-16. Instead give her a hug (and maybe a kiss on the cheek).

CHAPTER TEN

FRANCE

The author studied the French dances while he was in the French Army. Being the Director for the Fifth Armored Division Army theatre, then with the French and Belgian Boy Scouts, this gave many opportunities to do research on authentic dances, learning directly from the people.

One place where dance is still alive today is on the peninsula of Brittany (Bretagne), in the Pyrenees, and the Province or massive central.

Two dances from Brittany and one from the Bourree-country have been chosen for this book. The dance, "Eton," from Brittany, has always small steps, rather heavy because of the wooden shoes, saboes, which they have used for centuries. Today, some groups still use saboes but many others do not. The dance still reflects the movement as if shoes were used, however.

The second dance from Brittany is "Branle a' Six," dance for six. This is formed of two trios facing each other and dancing in unison.

The costumes are today more city costumes. The homemade ones are no longer available. The fabrics for the costumes and the handmade shoes specially constructed by the village cordonnier (shoemaker) are almost altogether gone now.

"La Bourree" is more light and is a mountaineer-type dynamic dance with typical 3/4 and 6/8 time. The boys are more active than the girls. This version is for one boy who solos frequently and two girls in a circle using the basic bourree step.

The best places today to see real French dances are at the festivals. One, the international festival of Folklore is held in

the summer at Biarritz. Nice holds celebrations, also, and from
time to time many other regions do, too. At the festivals, however, the French couples dances are severe and elegant with no
erotic emphasis. The men are courteous and they merely enjoy
dancing with the women.

The Alps, Brittany, the Pyrenees are the best and richest res-
ervoirs for the study of French dance folklore.

UN PIED DANS L'EAU
(A Foot in the Water)

SOURCE: Dance from the Vandee district south of Brittany. It is a type of Ridee which is a dance form common to Brittany. Learned by Anatol Joukowsky from French Boy Scouts.

MUSIC: Record — Disque Le Soleil 433-A 4/4 time. No introduction.

FORMATION: Two cpls. form a line. W are in middle and one M on each end. R hands on hips and link arms through neighbor's R. Free hands of M are on hips. Line faces in CW direction. Each person is a little behind one on L so that they do not stand abreast but on a diagonal. First M of one line is leleader.

```
        ↑ CW
     X   |
      O  |
         |  O
         |   X
```

STEPS: Walk, Two-step Directions are same for M and W.

PATTERN

Measures

Figure I. Walk and Sweep Foot

1   Taking 1 step to each ct., walk L R L. On ct. 4, sweep R ft. in arc out to R, ending behind L.

2   Step R (ct. 1). Step L beside R (ct. 2). Step fwd. R (ct. 3). Lift heel of R (modified hop) (ct. 4).

3-8   Repeat meas. 1-2 three more times (4 in all).

Figure II. Tapping

1   Cross L over R and tap L toe 4 times (leg straight). R heel is lifted before each tap (modified hop). On

this figure all face a little R of CW direction. Arms are still joined.

2   With small leap L, cross R over L and tap toe 4 times. L heel is lifted before each tap.

3-8   Repeat meas. 1-2 three more times (4 in all).

Figure III. Walk and Sweep Foot
1-16   Repeat Fig. I two times.

Figure IV. Tapping With Hand Motion
1   Repeat Fig II meas. 1. With elbow bent and close to side. R hand is extended fwd., chest height, palm up. On each tap forearm and hand are lowered to waist and returned to pos. L hand on hip.

2   Repeat Fig. II meas. 2. With elbow bent and close to side, extend L hand fwd., chest height, palm out. On each tap, move forearm and hand swd., R to L. R hand on hip.
Note: Originally a verse was sung throughout dance. At this point the words were saying, "Yes, my left foot does very well. No, my right is not so good."

3-8   Repeat Fig II meas. 1-2 three more times with the hand motions added.

Figure V. Walk and Sweep Foot
1-8   Repeat Fig. I. As action takes place, all sets move in so 1st M of each line links L arm through R arm of end M in next set. Leader does not link L arm so there is one break in circle.

Figure VI. Serpentine
1-16   Starting with L, do 32 two-steps (2 to a meas.). Leader serpentine line about room. Usually starts by leading line out to his L.

BRANLE a' SIX

SOURCE: Learned and danced in France by Anatol Jou-
               kowsky. Dance comes from Brittany. This de-
               scription fits the dance as done by the French
               Boy Scout Exhibition Group.

MUSIC: Record — Celtic Folk Dance Series, CFD-13A.

FORMATION: A set of 1 M between 2 W, facing another set of
               the same. Sets stand 10-12 ft. apart. If more than
               1 set dances, sets should line up side by side so
               lines are formed as in contra dances. M has fists
               on hips. W hook near arm through M arm. W
               free hand holds skirts. Whenever hands are free
               W hold skirts, M fists are on hips.

                    RW   LW
                      O——X——O

                      O——X——O
                    LW   RW

STEPS: *Walk, Skip.*

PATTERN

Measures

2 meas.   Introduction.

               Figure I. Forward and Clap
   1   Beg. R, walk fwd. 3 steps (1 to a ct.). Hop on R (ct.
               4). On hop, L knee is lifted high with ft. next to
               supporting leg.

   2   Repeat action of meas. 1, beg. L. On hop on L (ct. 4)
               M clap hands straight across.

   3-4   Repeat action of meas. 1-2 but moving bwd. to
               place. Omit the clap.

5-8   Repeat action of meas. 1-4.

Figure II. Elbow Turns

1-2   Beg. with hop on L and stepping on R, M and R W
       hook R elbows and with 8 skips make 2 CW turns.
       M free arm is raised out to side with elbow bent,
       palm fwd., R W free hand holds skirt. At same time,
       L W, holding skirts, make 2 small CCW circles in
       place (1 circle on 4 skips).
       Note: Any time a W is free during Fig II she turns
       in a small circle in place, holding skirts. L W always
       turns CCW when alone. R W turns CW. Any time
       M has elbow linked with W, his free arm is raised as
       described in meas. 1-2 (Fig. II).

3   M hook elbows with L W and make 1 CCW turn
       with 4 skips. R W make 1 CW turn alone. Hand
       pos. as in meas. 1-2 (Fig. II).

4   With 4 skips M cross set to take R elbows with Opp.
       L W. As M faces other set, this will be the W to his
       R. M pass L shoulders, fists on hips. W turn in place.

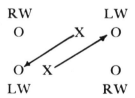

5-6   With 8 skips M turn Opp. L W twice with R elbows.
       R W turn alone.

7-8   With L elbows M turn Opp. R W once around with
       6 skips. L W turn alone. On last 2 skips M take ctr.
       pos. in opp. set. Repeat dance from beg. with M
       dancing in the set that was opp. him in Fig. I. At
       end of repeat M will be back with orig. ptrs. Con-
       tinue dance to end of music.

UNVERDOS
(Une vehr doe)
(One Against Two)

SOURCE: Unverdos is a Bourree, a principal dance form
               from Auvergne, France. It was learned by Anatol
               Joukowsky while at a school for French scout-
               masters in Shamarande, France in 1950.

MUSIC: Record — Folk Dances of the Provinces, Mercury
               MG 20338 (LP) Side 2, Band 1 (La Morianno —
               La Planese). 3/4 time.

FORMATION: Single circle composed of set of three (1 M be-
               tween 2 W) with all hands joined. One set is des-
               ignated as the Leading Set.

STEPS: *Basic Step:* Step R, bending knee (ct. 1). Step on ball of L next to R (ct. 2). Shift wt. back to R (ct. 3). Next step starts on L. Step on ct. 1 may be done in any direction. Always start on R for each figure.

Description same for M and W except where noted.

PATTERN

Measures

2   Introduction — stand in place, facing ctr.

Figure I

1-4   Turning to face a little L of Line of Direction, progress in LOD (CCW) with 4 basic steps (start on R).

5-8   Turning to face Reverse LOD (CW), dance 4 basic steps. Widen circle so arms are extended comfortably.

8-12   Dance 4 basic steps into ctr. As circle closes bring the hands up and bend the elbows until forearms of neighbors almost touch.

13-16 Dance 4 basic steps bkwd. to place. Hands are lowered as circle widens.

Figure II

1-4   M hook R elbow with R W and make 1 CW circle with 4 basic steps. M L arm is raised out to side with elbow bent, palm fwd. W R hand holds skirt. At same time, L W make 1 CCW circle, holding skirt with both hands.

5-8   M hook L elbows with L W and make 1 CCW turn on 4 basic steps. R W make 1 turn CW holding skirts.

9-16   Repeat action of meas. 1-8 (Fig. II).

1-32   *Repeat all from beginning.* Omit last 4 meas. Instead, M take W hands and each set of 3 turn to face LOD (CCW), still using basic step. L W of Leading Set form a connection by grasping L forearm of L W ahead. L W first raises L hand as a signal that she is starting. L W of set behind then grasp hold of forearm of L W of Leading Set. Continue until all are joined. Joining can continue into next figure if need be.

Figure III

1-4   Dance 4 basic steps in LOD(CCW).

5-8   On 4 basic steps M turn R W with R elbows once around. L W still has arm grasp.

9-12   Dance 4 basic steps in LOD(CCW).

13-16   On 4 basic steps, with inside hands joined, each set makes ½ turn CW to face RLOD(CW). R W back up. R W Leading Set start the arm grasp.

17-20   Dance 4 basic steps in RLOD(CW).

21-24   On 4 basic steps M turn L W with L elbows once around. R W still has arm grasp.

25-28   Dance 4 basic steps in RLOD(CW).

29-32   On 4 basic steps with inside hands joined, each set makes ¾ turn CCW to form original circle with all hands joined. L W back up.

1-32   *Repeat Action of Figure I and II.*

33-35   W step in so backs are to ctr. M faces ctr. W join nearest hand with M and hold skirt with outside hand.
Music stops.

2   Introduction — no action.

Figure IV

1-2   Dance 2 basic steps in place.

3-4   Change places on W basic steps. W turn under joined hands. R W turn $\frac{1}{2}$ L. L W turn $\frac{1}{2}$ R. M turn $\frac{1}{2}$ R as he crosses over to W side. M give lead to W for turn and drop joined hands after crossover is started.

5-6   Dance 2 basic steps in place. W join nearest hand with M. Outside hand hold skirt.

7-8   Change back to original place on 2 basic steps. W turn under joined hands. R W turn $\frac{1}{2}$ R. L W turn $\frac{1}{2}$ L. M still turn $\frac{1}{2}$ R. Again drop hands after crossover is started. Note: R W refers to W who started dance as R W even though pos. are changed for 4 meas.

9-16   Repeat action of meas. 1-8 (Fig. IV).

Figure V

1-4   Move into ctr. with 4 basic steps. Pos. is same as for start of Fig. IV.

5-8   Move out of ctr. with 4 basic steps.

9-16   On 8 basic steps form 2 circles. M in inside circle, W in outside circle. All face ctr. As M starts to move in, turn W under joined hands as in Fig. IV meas. 3-4. W join hands in outer circle. M continues in until able to join hands in inner circle. On meas. 15 and 16 M *only* claps on ct. 1.

17-18   *Men:* Dance 1 basic step to R and 1 to L.

19   Jump into air and land with L knee on floor. On jump progress a little to R.

20   Slap floor with palm of L near L knee. R hand is raised.

21-48   Rising, repeat action of meas. 17-20 (Fig. V) seven more times (8 in all).

17-24   *Women:* While man dances the above pattern, do following pattern. Circle CW with 8 basic steps.

25-28   W of each set hook R elbows and turn once on 4 basic steps.

29-32   Hook L elbows and turn once with 4 basic steps.

33-40   With hands rejoined in circle move CCW with 8 basic steps.

41-48   Repeat action of meas. 25-28 (Fig. V). End in single circle facing ctr. W shorten or lengthen steps so as to finish behind own M.

Figure VI

1-8   On 8 basic steps M backs out to place between his W. All sets join hands in big circle with only one break — between L W of Leading Set and W on her L.

9-35   Turning out to L, L W of Leading Set lead line in serpentine about hall using basic step. Dance to end of record. End W have free hands on hips.

INDEX

DANCE

A Books for Libraries Collection

Ashihara, Eiryo. **The Japanese Dance.** 1964

Bowers, Faubion. **Theatre in the East.** 1956

Brinson, Peter. **Background to European Ballet.** 1966

Causley, Marguerite. **An Introduction to Benesh Movement Notation.** 1967

Devi, Ragini. **Dances of India.** 1962

Duggan, Ann Schley, Jeanette Schlottmann and Abbie Rutledge. **The Teaching of Folk Dance.** Volume 1. 1948

————. **Folk Dances of Scandinavia.** Volume 2. 1948

————. **Folk Dances of European Countries.** Volume 3. 1948

————. **Folk Dances of the British Isles.** Volume 4. 1948

————. **Folk Dances of the United States and Mexico.** Volume 5. 1948

Duncan, Irma. **Duncan Dancer.** 1966

Dunham, Katherine. **A Touch of Innocence.** 1959

Emery, Lynne Fauley. **Black Dance in the United States from 1619 to 1970.** 1972

Fletcher, Ifan Kyrle, Selma Jeanne Cohen and Roger Lonsdale. **Famed for Dance.** 1960

Gautier, Théophile. **The Romantic Ballet as Seen by Théophile Gautier.** 1932

Genthe, Arnold. **Isadora Duncan.** 1929

Hall, J. Tillman. **Dance! A Complete Guide to Social, Folk, & Square Dancing.** 1963

Jackman, James L., ed. **Fifteenth Century Basse Dances.** 1964

Joukowsky, Anatol M. **The Teaching of Ethnic Dance.** 1965

Kahn, Albert Eugene. **Days with Ulanova.** 1962

Karsavina, Tamara. **Theatre Street.** 1950

Lawson, Joan. **European Folk Dance.** 1953

Martin, John. **The Dance.** 1946

Sheets-Johnstone, Maxine. **The Phenomenology of Dance.** 1966